Thinking Out Loud

Anna

Preface

Annette R. Fraser is a truth-speaker with a fearless heart and a gift for turning reflection into revelation. With a voice shaped by experience and a spirit rooted in wisdom, she brings raw honesty, gentle strength, and soulful clarity to every conversation she starts.

Thinking Out Loud isn't just a title—it's a movement. A rhythm of thought, feeling, and fearless self-expression.

The author doesn't just write to be heard.

She writes to connect.

To stir something real.

To remind you that you are never alone in your thoughts… or your awakening.

Welcome to her world of insight, empowerment, and radical honesty.

This is Anna… thinking out loud.

Table of Contents

About the Author

My name is Annette—but those around me call me Anna. It's the name that feels most like home and the name I answer to with a smile. It's a softer echo of who I am, shaped by love, laughter, and life's lessons.

That's why at the end of every reflection, you'll hear me say, "This is Anna, thinking out loud." It's not just a sign-off—it's a gentle whisper from my heart to yours.

Professionally, I am a Certified Neuro-Linguistic Programmer and a Multi-Model Approach Therapist. I integrate the most effective elements of renowned counselling and psychotherapy models into a unique, tried-and-tested approach designed to help individuals overcome challenges, heal, grow, and step fully into their purpose.

My work is centred on guiding people toward wholeness, resolution, and personal empowerment.

Personally, I am a dynamic blend of strength, loyalty, depth, and humour. I'm analytical yet compassionate, highly driven yet deeply playful. I embrace my complexities—a simple woman with a beautifully intricate mind, much like many others navigating this world.

I thrive on connecting with like-minded individuals who share my energy and curiosity about the human experience. I love exploring inner personalities and perspectives, always standing firm in my beliefs but never in competition with anyone. My mission is to uplift, empower, and inspire—one conversation, one insight, and one breakthrough at a time.

Dedication

"Success is to be measured not so much by the position that one has reached in life as by the obstacles which he has overcome."

—Booker T. Washington.

This quote has walked with me through the fire, through the breakthroughs, and into this very moment—where I now have the honour of sharing Thinking Out Loud with you.

This book is a reflection of every mountain I've climbed, every lesson I've learned, and the courage it takes to say things out loud—especially when the world would rather you whisper.

I could not have arrived here alone.

To my son—Kyle, my heart in human form—Thank you for your unwavering wisdom, for being my rock, and for being the heartbeat of my purpose and strength. Every day, you remind me of the limitless power within me. I am endlessly in awe of you and the incredible soul you are.

To my big sister—Maria, who balances me with love and unwavering truth—your presence has always grounded me.

To my Sistas, who have been my lieutenants and consiglieri throughout my life. My steady shelter in every storm.

To my Family, whose roots run deep, thank you for being my anchor, my safe place and the hands that lifted me when standing felt too heavy, and to my few dearest friends who have loved me without condition—thank you for holding space for my growth, for cheering when I couldn't, and for reminding me who I am when I forgot.

And to Isaiah and Nyla—my newest inspirations—may this guide be a legacy of light, love, and the power of finding your voice.

Fearless.

Flawless.

Fierce.

And fully

Prepared

Rise in Power Sis

Life as a woman is a journey filled with complexities, triumphs, heartbreaks, and lessons—each shaping us into who we are meant to be. Through the pages of this book, I share my thoughts on love, relationships, self-value, the power of a positive mindset, and the importance of mental well-being. These are the cornerstones of a fulfilled life, and if you take nothing else from these words, I hope you take this:

You are divine. You are limitless. You are rooted in purpose.

I won't claim to have all the answers, nor do I believe I can single-handedly change the world. But what I can do—what I must do—is live my truth, share my experiences, and help you see the power that already exists within you. If I can guide you, even in the smallest way, toward seeing yourself in a new light—toward saving yourself from self-doubt, self-sabotage, or the weight of expectations—then I will have done what I was meant to do.

My goal is growth—mine and yours. My desire is empowerment—not just for myself, but for every woman who has ever questioned her worth. And my religion? Love. Love for self, love for others, and love for the journey that makes us who we are. While this guide is designed to empower women, men will find valuable insights that can strengthen their relationships and deepen their understanding of a woman's needs and lived experience.

So, as you read these words, take what resonates, challenge what doesn't, and most importantly, open yourself to the possibility that everything you've been searching for has been inside you all along.

Let's begin...

CHILL!

I created and copyrighted the acronym CHILL—Choose Holistic Invaluable Life Lessons—because I wholeheartedly embrace and live by this mindset. I believe that with the right perspective, anything is possible, achievable, and within reach.

More often than not, I close my talks with the simple yet powerful phrase, "Just CHILL." And when I say it, I mean exactly this: choose growth, embrace wisdom, and approach life with a sense of clarity and purpose. CHILL isn't just a word—it's a way of thinking, living, and thriving.

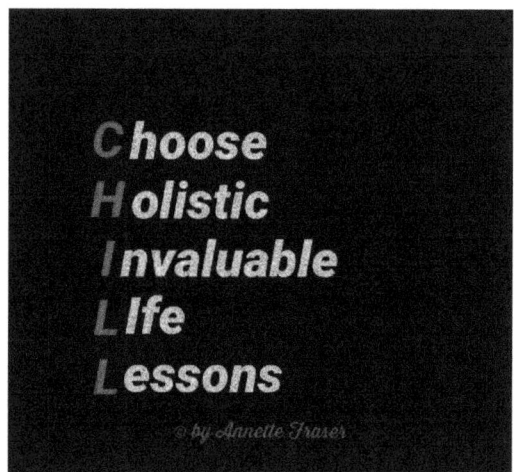

The Essence of Who You Are

Like your reflection in the mirror, let the world see the essence of who you truly are—your real, unfiltered self. Not the carefully edited version you present to others because let's be honest—that must be exhausting.

Take a step back and intentionally edit yourself—not for the world, but for you. Choose to stand tall, to save yourself, to refine and improve, and most importantly, to believe in your own strength and capabilities.

Within you lies an Empress waiting to be unveiled. Set her free. Whatever made you dim your light or hide your true self—it's time to forgive it, release it, and move forward with confidence.

Life is about change, and that's a good thing. You shouldn't be the same person you were a year ago, six months ago, or even a few weeks ago. If you are, it means you've stood still, and growth has passed you by. Instead, empower yourself to evolve every single day—through listening, learning, reading, speaking, and embracing the experiences that nurture your mental, spiritual, and emotional expansion.

Be smarter. Be wiser. Be remarkably brave. Let go of insecurities and step into your full potential. When you finally embrace the depth of who you are, others will admire you—not for the image you project, but for the true content of your soul.

Yes, we all stumble. We all fall. But the power lies in getting up, standing firm, and stepping forward with purpose. And that journey—that transformation—will be nothing short of extraordinary if only you believe in the essence of who you truly are.

This is Anna, Thinking Out Loud!

There's one letter in
the alphabet that
controls your entire
existence....
'U'
It's always 'U'
It has always been 'U'
It will always be
'U'

This is Anna, Thinking Out Loud

A Difficult Relationship: Acceptance & a Spiritual Response

After a deep group discussion about a difficult relationship marked by betrayal, hurt, anger, and resentment, I found myself wondering—why do these emotions remain so powerful, even years after the relationship has ended? How can something that is no longer physically present still hold such a grip on the heart and mind?

It became clear that while the relationship had ended, emotional ties had not been completely severed. One party continued to engage in harmful behaviours, while the other felt powerless to break free from the cycle of pain. The past remained alive in the present, and with it, the weight of unresolved emotions.

The Power of Acceptance

Acceptance is about seeing things as they truly are in the present moment. It is not about approval or justification—it is about acknowledgment. Too often, we resist accepting situations we have deemed unacceptable, believing that acceptance equates to condoning what happened. But acceptance is not about passing judgment—neither positive nor negative. It is simply recognising reality for what it is, without distortion.

Many of us suffer because we refuse to accept experiences from the past, replaying them in our minds with rigid, unforgiving narratives. We reinforce our own suffering by holding onto "what should have been" instead of embracing "what is."

While we may not have control over everything in our lives, we do have influence over our responses. True acceptance is the understanding that some things cannot be changed and others can only be changed with time, effort, and patience. Patience itself is a form of wisdom—an acknowledgment that life unfolds in its own time, not always according to our expectations.

This is Anna, Thinking Out Loud

The Role of Spirituality in Healing

When we open our minds and hearts, real change can begin. Healing comes not only from understanding ourselves but also from embracing something greater—Spirituality.

Spirituality can be a profound source of emotional and mental strength. It nurtures resilience through faith, hope, forgiveness, kindness, empathy, compassion, and prayer. These elements are not just abstract concepts; they have a tangible impact on our well-being.

To be spiritual is to embark on a journey of self-discovery, to seek meaning in our experiences, and to rebuild ourselves after life's challenges. When we incorporate spirituality into our daily lives— whether through mindfulness, meditation, or simple acts of kindness—we create a space for healing, peace, and personal transformation.

By embracing spirituality, we equip ourselves with the tools to navigate stress, anxiety, depression, and moments of hopelessness. It becomes a guiding force that allows us to find balance even in difficult times.

Moving Forward

True acceptance and spiritual growth does not happen overnight, but they are powerful forces for change. Letting go of resentment, practicing patience, and embracing a spiritual approach to life can free us from the burdens of the past.

When we learn to accept, we empower ourselves. When we nurture our spirit, we heal. And when we allow change, we grow.

The Path to Self-Discovery and Spiritual Awareness

As your spirituality deepens, you will uncover a greater sense of purpose, inner peace, and emotional resilience. It will help you navigate stress, face challenges with strength, stay grounded in your truth, and communicate more effectively with those who matter most.

Spiritual awareness also strengthens your intuition. Trusting your instincts is not paranoia—it's wisdom. Your body and mind naturally pick up on negative energy and subtle vibrations. If something deep inside you whispers that a situation or person isn't right, listen to it. Your intuition is a gift; never discredit it.

While you may not always have control over what happens to you, you do have control over how you respond. And in mastering your mindset, you master change—rather than allowing it to master you. As Sri Ram wisely said, *"Sometimes you cannot control what happens to you, but you can control your attitude towards what happens to you."*

A wise woman walks through life with clarity and confidence. She chooses peace over conflict, but she also chooses never to be anyone's victim.

You don't have to agree with me, but as usual…

This is Anna, Thinking Out Loud!

Self Help Exercise

Over the next few weeks, each time a self-critical thought arises, pause and reflect — awareness is the first step to change.

How do you react to criticism of yourself?

Write down the supportive things you can say to yourself or do for yourself.

_____
_____
_____
_____
_____
_____
_____
_____

Write down the supportive things you can say to yourself or do for yourself.

_____
_____
_____
_____
_____
_____

See if you can decrease your critical comments and increase your supportive statements. Write a few here:

_____

_____

_____

_____

_____

_____

This is Anna, Thinking Out Loud!

"Don't Worry"

Does this phrase frustrate you as much as it does me?

When people say *"**Don't worry,**"* they often mean well, but let's be honest—it's rarely helpful. Imagine someone facing eviction. Saying, "Don't worry, things will work out," doesn't pay their arrears or put a roof over their head. Unless you're offering a solution—like covering their rent or giving them a place to stay—telling someone not to worry is meaningless. In fact, it can feel dismissive, making them feel even more alone in their struggle.

Worry, in itself, isn't always a bad thing. It's a natural response to challenges, a signal that something needs attention. Short-term worry can be useful—it pushes us to take action, find solutions, and problem-solve effectively. The key is not letting worry consume you but using it as motivation to tackle what's in front of you.

That said, *long-term worry can be harmful*. It drains energy, clouds judgment, and leads to stress. So, while it's okay to acknowledge your concerns, it's equally important to develop strategies to manage them—whether that's seeking support, making a plan, or practicing mindfulness.

Instead of saying, ***"Don't worry,"*** let's offer real support, solutions, or even just a listening ear. Because sometimes, people don't need empty reassurances—they need action, understanding, and a way forward.

This is Anna, Thinking Out Loud!

The Power of the Past

They fuck you up, your mum and dad; They may not mean to, but
they do. They fill you with the faults they had
And add some extra just for You.
But they were fucked up in their turn By old style fools in hats and
coats
Who half the time were sloppy-stern
And half at one another's throats.
Man hands on misery to man
It deepens like a coastal shelf
Get out, as early as you can
—Phillip Larkin, Poet

This small extract piece from the poem by Philip Larkin, opens his famously raw and haunting piece "This Be The Verse." From a past and its power perspective, it speaks volumes about how deeply the past shapes us—especially the legacy passed down through generations of family and society.

Let's break it down:

"They fuck you up, your mum and dad/ They may not mean to, but they do."

This opening hits hard—it's blunt and unapologetic. Larkin is confronting the emotional and psychological inheritance we receive

19

from our parents. The key here is the idea that harm is often unintentional, yet no less damaging. Even the people who love us can pass on trauma.

"They fill you with the faults they had/And add some extra just for You."

This highlights how personal histories carry emotional residue: traits, insecurities, and learned behaviours—often without conscious awareness. Not only do we inherit our parents' struggles, but we also accumulate new ones shaped by our unique experiences in the world. It's the compounding effect of generational pain.

"But they were fucked up in their turn / By old style fools in hats and coats."

Now we zoom out. Larkin traces the damage even further back—to previous generations and perhaps societal institutions or cultural norms ("old style fools in hats and coats"). He suggests a cycle of dysfunction—where each generation, knowingly or not, is shaped by the failures and contradictions of the one before.

"Who half the time were sloppy-stern/And half at one another's throats."

This paints a picture of inconsistent parenting and unstable relationships. It shows the confusion children grow up with — one minute, there's discipline (often rigid or irrational), and the next minute, there's chaos or conflict. The past here is not just about individuals, but also the environment they create.

"Man hands on misery to man / It deepens like a coastal shelf."

This is the poem's most profound statement. The image of a coastal shelf is powerful—suggesting that as time passes, the weight of inherited pain gets deeper, more layered, and harder to escape. Misery isn't just personal; it becomes a legacy—something we pass down almost like an heirloom.

Final Thoughts: The Past's Inescapable Gravity

From this view, the poem suggests that the past wields immense power—it shapes who we are, often beneath our awareness. Larkin's message is grim but truthful: unless consciously interrupted, emotional pain repeats itself through generations.

It's not a poem that offers hope — but it's a clarion call to awareness. And awareness, in itself, is a starting point for breaking cycles.

This is Anna, Thinking Out Loud

A Guide to Self-Compassion

Embracing yourself. Accepting yourself. Forgiving yourself. Learning to say no. Recognising when enough is enough. These are not just acts of self-care; they are declarations of your value and self-worth.

That inner critical voice? The one that tries to tear you down? It's time to silence it. When it starts whispering doubts, tell it firmly: **"Not today!" Today, I choose me.**

Today, I will light my favourite scented candles, go for a run, enjoy a glass of red wine or Chai latte, have an early night, and switch off my phone. Because self-compassion isn't just about thoughts—it's about action. It's about treating yourself with the same kindness, patience, and love that you so freely give to others.

Think about it—if someone you love was struggling with stress, anxiety, loss, or self-doubt, how would you respond? You'd offer comfort, support, and reassurance. So why wouldn't you do the same for yourself?

Start implementing self-kindness today. Surround yourself with people, places, and experiences that nurture your spirit. Feed your soul with positivity, and watch how that energy transforms you.

My self-compassion starts with *me*.

I love to live. I love to laugh. I love to sing. I love to dance.

I love *ME!* I will never apologise for being *Bold, Beautiful, Wonderful Me!*

So what compassionate words can you tell yourself? Write them here:

_____
_____
_____
_____
_____
_____
_____
_____
_____
_____

The moral of the story is simple: Be good to yourself. You deserve it!

This is Anna, Thinking Out Loud!

An Important Lesson

They say the Universe gives back what you put into it. Keep this in mind in all your relationships—personal and professional.

Words spoken in anger often reveal what's buried in the heart, even if just for a moment. But that moment can leave a lasting mark. Whether those words linger in someone's conscious mind—playing on repeat—or get tucked away in their subconscious, only to resurface when triggered, the damage has already been done.

Think of it like an unwanted tattoo. No matter how much you regret getting it, it doesn't just disappear. You can try to cover it up with makeup or hide it under clothing, but it's still there, waiting to be revealed. Words, especially hurtful ones, are the same. A verbal assault can be just as painful as a physical one—sometimes even worse. While physical wounds heal, cruel words can echo in the mind long after they've been spoken.

So, work hard to be the best version of yourself. Treat others with fairness, kindness, and compassion. Always be mindful of your words because what you say has the power to either strengthen or destroy the relationships in your life.

Spiteful, careless, or shameful words are not just a reflection of the person receiving them; they reflect who you are in that moment. If you speak with anger and cruelty, don't be surprised when the world responds in kind. That is an important lesson.

The moral of the story?

Your words have power. They can uplift, heal, and inspire—or they can break, wound, and discourage. A single sentence can be the difference between life and death, hope and despair, joy and sorrow.

So before you speak, pause. Think about the weight of your words. Because once spoken, they cannot be undone.

This is Anna, Thinking out Loud!

The One-Sided Conversation is Exhausting...

I recently listened to a group conversation, and *cue the eye roll* the topic, yet again, was relationships. And not just any conversation about relationships, but the typical one: a one-sided, male-dominated discussion about what a woman must do to keep a man.

The list of "must-dos" went something like this:

1. Trust him—Don't go through his phone or ask too many questions about its content.

2. Always meet his sexual needs—Give him sex whenever he wants, or he 'may' get it elsewhere.

3. Stay attractive—Keep yourself looking fine, or he'll lose interest.

4. Give him space—Don't be clingy or needy.

5. Be able to cook—Because, apparently, the way to a man's heart is through his stomach.

The list goes on... Blah, blah, blah!

And here we go again, ladies—another reminder of what we need to be doing, as if relationships don't require mutual effort. Tiring, right?

But here's the part that may surprise you: I actually agree with most of these points, its reality of life. But keep reading for clarity...

The Real Question

Why is it that conversations like these rarely discuss what a man should be doing to deserve and keep a good woman—especially one who checks all the boxes on their precious little list?

Spoiler alert! Women want the same things that men expect from them. Yes, we want men who:

✓ Have good hygiene and a great smile.

✓ Keep their bodies in decent shape.

✓ Are financially stable.

✓ Possess an intelligent and stimulating mind.

✓ Show masculinity through good deeds & kindness.

Let's be real, fellas. You want a woman with a tiny waist and a flat stomach, but your own stomach looks like you're carrying a set of full-term twins? Where's the justice?

Check Your Offerings Before You Start Demanding

Now, before anyone gets triggered, I'm not saying relationships are only about physical appearances. This is just one example to highlight the imbalance.

Here's the truth: Your worth as a man is demonstrated through action, not dictated through demands. If you feel the need to constantly tell a woman what she should be doing, chances are, you're fishing in the wrong pond, Brotha.

Let me break it down for you:

If you're casting your net in the deep, abundant waters of the Mediterranean, you better be equipped for the catch. If your net is worn out and can only hold small fish, how dare you demand a woman hand over her haul of lobster when all you're bringing in is sardines?

The Bottom Line

Integrity, decency, fairness, and respect—these are the bare minimum requirements for any successful partnership. If both partners bring these qualities to the table, maybe, just maybe, future conversations about relationships won't be so damn one-sided.

This is Anna and I'm just Thinking out Loud!

Hindsight: The Wisdom We Wish We Had Sooner

Definition: "Understanding a situation or event only after it has happened or developed."

Hindsight is a powerful thing—but wouldn't it be even more powerful if we could recognise its lessons before disaster strikes?

When things fall apart—whether in relationships, friendships, or life decisions—we often look back and say, "If only I had paid attention to that red flag," or "If only I knew then what I know now, things would have been different."

But hindsight, by its very nature, comes after the fact. And because it arrives late to the party, we either tolerate harmful behaviour, mirror them or ignore them completely while trying to make sense of the situation. By the time we truly see things for what they are, we may have already invested too much time, energy, and emotion into something that was never good for us to begin with.

What If We Had 'Pre-Hindsight?'

Imagine if we had the ability to recognise patterns, behaviours, and motives before they caused damage—if we could pause at the beginning of an experience, observe the unfolding events, and make an informed decision about whether to continue or walk away. Let's call it Pre-Hindsight (While "pre-hindsight" isn't a standard word, it's a creative combination).

If we possessed this kind of foresight, we wouldn't have to learn the hard way. Instead of falling into toxic cycles, we would have the clarity and strength to set boundaries, challenge unhealthy patterns, and protect our emotional well-being before things spiral out of control.

From Hindsight to Foresight

The reality is, hindsight only helps us after the lesson has been learned. But what if we could develop foresight instead?

For those with less life experience, the best tool to avoid future regret is **open communication**—learning to ask the right questions, trust your intuition, and not dismiss uncomfortable feelings. For those who have been through life's ups and downs, wisdom teaches us to recognise patterns, understand triggers, and take action before things turn into an "if only" moment.

Hindsight is a teacher. Foresight is a superpower. The sooner we learn to recognise early signs, set boundaries, and trust our instincts, the fewer regrets we'll carry. So while we can't change the past, we can use what we've learned to create a better, stronger future—one where we don't have to look back and say, "I should have known."

This is Anna, Thinking Out Loud!

Echoes of Wisdom: Inspiration from the Greats"

"But behavior in the human being is sometimes a defense, a way of concealing motives and thoughts, as language can be a way of hiding your thoughts and preventing communication."

—Abraham Maslow

"Shared joy is a double joy; shared sorrow is half a sorrow."

—Swedish Proverb

"It is easier to forgive an enemy than to forgive a friend."

—William Blake

"The pendulum of the mind alternates between sense and nonsense, not between right and wrong."

—Carl Jung

"Once you make a decision, the universe conspires to make it happen."

—Ralph Waldo Emerson, Poet

"If you don't like something, change it. If you can't change it, change your attitude."

—Maya Angelou, Poet

"The curious paradox is that when I accept myself just as I am, then I can change."

—Carl R. Rogers, Psychologist

"There is only one corner of the universe you can be certain of improving, and that's your own self."

—Aldus Huxley, Philosopher

Empowered by History: The Words That Shape Us

"Failing is a crucial part of success. Every time you
fail and get back up, you practice perseverance, which
is the key to life. Your strength comes in your ability to
recover."

—Michelle Obama, Former First Lady of the
United States

"My friend…care for your psyche… know thyself, for
once we know ourselves, we may learn how to care
for ourselves."

—Socrates, Philosopher

"Progress is impossible without change, and those who cannot
change their minds cannot change anything."

—George Bernard Shaw, Playwright

"I am enough of an artist to draw freely upon my imagination.
Imagination is more important than knowledge. Knowledge is
limited. Imagination encircles the world."

—Albert Einstein, Nobel Prize Winning Physicist

"A ship is always safe at the shore—but that is not what it is built for."

—Albert Einstein, Nobel Prize Winning Physicist

"No one can make you feel inferior without your consent."

—Eleanor Roosevelt, Former First Lady

Lessons from History's Giants

"It's easy to stand in the crowd but it takes courage
to stand alone."

— Mahatma Gandhi, Lawyer and social Activist

"If you do not study history, you are doomed to repeat it.' 'You
cannot choose your circumstances, but you can choose how to
respond to them."

—Aphorism

"Impermanence does not necessarily lead to suffering. What
makes us suffer is wanting things to be permanent when they are
not."

—Thich Nhat Hanh

Now think about the power of your own thoughts. Write about an
area in your life that you would like to be bolder, stronger, wiser.
What would you say or do?

_____

_____

_____

_____

_____

☐ Notice when you're being hard on yourself, you deserve your compassion.

☐ Whenever you catch yourself speaking unkindly to yourself, write it down. This is how we begin to shift the narrative.

Now look at your list, it's a call for action – don't overthink it!

This is Anna, Thinking Out Loud!

Overthinking doesn't
solve problems- it
creates them!
Stress is a global
epidemic,
So laugh more, run
often and mind your own
business….

This is Anna, Thinking Out Loud

One Conversation, One Insight, One Breakthrough

Sometimes, transformation begins in the most unassuming moments. A simple conversation, a passing comment, or a single phrase spoken at the right time can be the spark that ignites an entirely new way of thinking.

How many times have we carried the weight of self-doubt, believing we are not enough, only to have one conversation that shifts everything? A friend's reminder of our strength. A mentor's wisdom that makes us pause. A stranger's words that echo in our hearts.

One insight—that's all it takes. The realisation, that you are not defined by past mistakes, nor by the expectations placed upon you. The understanding that you have always had the power to rewrite your story. That moment when you see yourself clearly, beyond the limiting beliefs that once held you captive.

And then, the breakthrough. The moment you decide to stop waiting for permission. To stop apologising for taking up space. To stop settling for less than you deserve. This is the moment when you reclaim your voice, your worth, and your future.

Never underestimate the power of a single exchange. Pay attention to the wisdom life places before you. Stay open to the lessons hidden in everyday conversations. Sometimes, the words you need most will arrive in unexpected ways—and when they do, let them guide you to your next breakthrough.

You are always one moment away from stepping into the person you were meant to be...

This is Anna, Thinking Out Loud

Make This Week a Great One

No matter what challenges come your way, decide right now that this will be a blessed, peaceful, and prosperous week. Declare it, believe it, and refuse to accept anything less!

Smile—and the world will smile back.

This week, choose to be in spaces where your energy is reciprocated, valued, and nurtured. Go where you are understood, embraced, and appreciated—because that's where you will truly thrive.

Happiness isn't something you rent—it's something you own. My joy lives rent-free in my mind because I've learned to recognise and appreciate my resilience. And if you do the same, yours will too.

You are capable, strong, and smart. You can accomplish anything you set your mind to. Every person carries within them the knowledge and ideas to make their life better. So instead of focusing on weaknesses and fear, focus on your strengths.

This is what we call Solution-Based Thinking—the practice of creating your own solutions, on your own terms. Sometimes, all you need is a reminder of how strong you already are. Think about the obstacles you've already overcome.

Think about the moments when you refused to give up. Think about the moments you fell down but got back up again.

You are here. You are still standing. And that is worth celebrating.

So this week, step into your power—smile, move with confidence, and watch how the world responds in kind.

Let's get it!

This is Anna, Thinking Out Loud!

Building Confidence Exercise

1. Keep a Journal and commit yourself to spending at least ten minutes a day, every day journaling and then reflect on it at the end of each week. Notice how you feel.

2. Think about what difference it would make in your life if you knew you could achieve anything—write all about this in your Journal.

3. What does confidence mean to you—what would you do differently if you were confident? Write it on the lines below.

_____

_____

_____

_____

_____

_____

_____

_____

_____

_____

4. Commit yourself to behaving more confidently—even if it feels like an act. Soon enough the confidence will become part of your personality and will start to show up every day.

This is Anna, Thinking Out Loud!

I Solemnly Swear to Empower Myself

To create meaningful, positive changes in life, we must make a commitment to ourselves—to take action, to embrace growth, and to honour our own journey.

Here are some powerful pledges to help guide the way:

- I empower myself to focus on what is good in my life and what is beautiful about me.
- I dedicate myself to doing whatever it takes to create the changes I know I need and want in my life.
- I challenge myself to embrace my fears rather than avoid them.
- I allow myself to sit with discomfort, knowing that facing my thoughts and feelings is a step toward healing.
- I practice patience with myself as I explore new approaches and pathways to growth.
- I forgive myself for setbacks and mistakes, knowing they are part of my journey—not the end of it.
- I prioritise the three R's—Rest, Relaxation, and Recuperation—so I have the energy to achieve my goals.

- I welcome the support I need to help me find inner peace and balance.
- I acknowledge and celebrate my efforts, no matter how small, because every step forward matters.

These are my pledges. If they resonate with you, make them yours—or create your own! The power to transform your life begins with You.

This is Anna, Thinking Out Loud!

The Energy of a Relationship: Love, Respect & Balance

Relationships

Definition:

1. The way in which two or more people or things are connected, or the state of being connected; the way in which two or more people or groups regard and behave towards each other.

2. An emotional attachment and sexual association between two people. (Concise Oxford English Dictionary)

When a relationship becomes unsupportive or oppressive, over time, you will feel drained—physically, emotionally, and mentally. Eventually, you'll lose the energy and motivation to continue investing in it. But here's the truth: learning to stand up for yourself, even if it means the relationship ends, can unlock a strength and motivation you never knew you had.

If you fear change, rejection, or abandonment, or if jealousy, guilt, or insecurity consume the relationship, then an unhealthy imbalance has taken root. These emotions can deplete you, leaving little room to give, receive, or experience the love and support you truly deserve.

Both individuals in the relationship must take responsibility for themselves. If only one person carries the weight of emotional labour while the other takes without giving back, the balance will always be unequal and unsustainable. The Great Book teaches that a woman should respect her husband, and a man should create an environment of love for his wife. When both partners commit to these principles, the relationship naturally fosters harmony. The more love He pours into Her, the more respect She gives Him. The more respect He feels, the more love He wants to give in return. This cycle of love and respect fuels a strong, lasting bond.

The key is to acknowledge both love and fear within the relationship and to actively find ways to respect each other's differences. When mutual love and respect exist, the relationship becomes a place of growth, trust, and genuine connection.

What can you do to further strengthen the connection in your relationship?

What can your partner do to further strengthen the connection in your relationship? Write it here:

This is Anna, Thinking Out Loud!

Intellectual Expectations

When I think of intellectual expectations in a relationship, I want to emphasise mutual growth, understanding, and respect. Reassure your partner while conveying to them that intellectual engagement is a way to enrich the relationship and should not feel or be seen as a burden or demand. Intellectual expectations in a relationship is not about superiority but about growing together.

Encourage Open Communication: Let your partner know that it's okay to talk about things that matter to them intellectually and to discuss topics they may not fully understand. By encouraging this kind of dialogue, both partners can grow together without anyone feeling overwhelmed or inadequate. It's about making the relationship a safe space for learning and questioning.

This is not about ignoring your own set of standards or sacrificing your intellectual integrity....

Having intellectual expectations in a relationship doesn't mean that neither you nor your partner have to change who you are or give up the things you love. Instead, it's about creating an environment where you both feel comfortable challenging your ideas, learning new things, and growing together. Respect who you both are and where you are in your journey, and be excited to keep exploring and learning together, without any pressure. The goal is for both of you to feel inspired and supported, not to meet some external standard, but to grow in ways that are meaningful to you both.

This is Anna, Thinking Out Loud!

A man who does not
know where He is
going, cannot lead you
anywhere.....

The Chosen Ones: Friendship, Peace and Knowing When to Let Go

There comes a time in life—especially as we grow, heal, and evolve — when we begin to understand that friendship is no small thing. It's not just about who makes you laugh or who's known you the longest. It's about who truly sees you. Who claps for you when you win. Who holds space for your heart when it's heavy. Who walks beside you not just in the sunlight, but in the storm.

As we journey through life—especially when our parents are no longer physically here—our chosen friends often become our emotional anchors. They are the family we gather along the way. The ones who show up without being asked. The ones who know the sound of your silence. The ones who remind you of your strength when you start to forget it.

Those are the rare ones. The real ones. The keepers.

But let's talk about the other side, too.

Because not everyone who calls you friend, is.

Some people are drawn to your light but can't stand your shine.

Some smile in your face, but wince at your wins.

Some only come around when they need your warmth, but never stay long enough to offer any of their own.

Let's call that what it is: Draining. Distracting. Unaligned.

And here's the truth that sets you free:

You don't owe anyone permanent space in your life just because you share a history.

Friendship should never feel like emotional labour.

If it steals your peace, dims your spirit, or makes you second-guess your worth—it's not a friendship. It's an attachment that's expired.

It's okay to outgrow people.

It's okay to love someone and still walk away.

It's okay to choose yourself—and your peace—over the performance of loyalty.

There is nothing wrong with having a loving heart and strong boundaries.

This is Anna, Thinking Out Loud

Value What Nourishes You

Be intentional about who gets your time, your energy, your laughter, your vulnerability. These are sacred offerings. They belong in safe hands.

Surround yourself with people who:

- celebrate your evolution
- tell you the truth with love
- want to see you win without needing to dim your light
- offer consistency, not just convenience
- love you in your becoming, not just in who you used to be

Because that kind of friendship? It fuels the soul. It strengthens your walk. It reminds you that you are not alone.

Closing Reflection: The Garden of You

Think of your life as a garden.

Not every plant is meant to stay. Some were beautiful for a season, and that was enough.

Some were weeds—taking more than they gave.

But some... some are your perennial blessings. They bloom with you, year after year. Nurture those.

Walk gently. But walk wisely.

Not everyone is for you—and that's a blessing, too.

Your energy is a gift—don't spend it proving your worth. Peace is power; protect it like your favourite secret.

This is Anna, Thinking Out Loud

Affirmation: I Choose Peace Over Performance

I welcome friendships that water my spirit,

Not ones that drain my light.

I am not afraid to walk alone, if it means protecting my peace.

I am loved, even in silence.

I am supported, even when I release.

I choose depth over drama.

I choose honesty over history.

I choose peace over performance.

And I trust —

That the ones who are truly for me

Will always know where to find me:

Rooted, Rising, and **Free**.

This is Anna, Thinking Out Loud

The Power of Forgiveness

Have you ever struggled to forgive yourself for staying in a relationship long past its expiration date? Or wrestled with the idea of forgiving someone who deeply wronged you?

If we truly want to embrace forgiveness, we must first release the emotional burdens that block our personal growth—anger, resentment, bitterness, and helplessness. These emotions may feel justified, even necessary, but they often do more harm to us than the person who caused the pain.

Forgiving can feel like an injustice, as if letting go means excusing the hurt or minimising your pain. But in reality, forgiveness is not about the other person(s)—it's about freeing yourself. It is the first step toward healing, toward reclaiming your power, and ultimately, toward forgiving yourself.

Healing isn't linear. Just when you think you've moved on, an unexpected trigger can bring the pain rushing back, forcing you to start the process over again. That's normal. Forgiveness is not a one-time decision but a commitment to release the weight of the past—again and again—until it no longer controls you.

Holding onto resentment doesn't just weigh on your mind—it weighs on your body. Studies show that stress weakens the immune system, leaving us vulnerable to illness, fatigue, and emotional exhaustion. When we cling to anger and hostility, we are choosing to carry pain that could be put down.

But let's be clear: forgiving is not forgetting. It does not mean dismissing the hurt, allowing toxic people back into your life, or excusing harmful behaviour. It means refusing to let the pain define you. It means making peace with the past so that it no longer poisons your present.

It won't happen overnight, but with time, effort, and self-compassion, you'll reach a moment when the pain doesn't cut as deep—when the weight is lighter, and your heart feels freer. That's when you'll know: forgiveness has taken root, and peace is finally within reach.

Set your own path and move on. It's a journey but the end destination is self-growth, and I promise you that it will be rewarding.

You deserve that peace. Choose it.

How do you define forgiveness?

_____
_____
_____
_____
_____
_____
_____

What will you need to do to work towards forgiving someone who has wronged you?

_____
_____
_____
_____
_____
_____

Now, What will you need to do to work towards forgiving yourself?

_____
_____
_____
_____
_____
_____

This is Anna, Thinking Out Loud

Influence Begins with You

Relationships shape every aspect of life—whether personal or professional. From your parents, partners and friends to colleagues, mentors, and even the barista who makes your morning coffee, the connections we form influence our experiences. But the most important relationship of all? The one you have with yourself.

How you manage your thoughts, emotions, and self-worth directly impacts how you navigate relationships with others. Self-awareness, self-love, and self-respect set the foundation for how you give and receive in all aspects of life. If you are thoughtful, kind, and compassionate, those qualities will naturally extend to those around you, inspiring the same in return—especially in children, peers, and those who look up to you. **It all starts with you.**

Influencing others doesn't require titles, degrees, or credentials—it requires character. The willingness to learn, to grow, to communicate with clarity, and to lead with integrity. When you cultivate empathy, acceptance, authenticity, self-compassion, and basic human decency, you not only strengthen your own emotional well-being but also create an environment where relationships can thrive.

Your energy is contagious. The way you carry yourself, the way you speak, the way you treat others—it all has an impact. So, if you want better relationships, a better life, and a more positive influence on the world around you, start by becoming the best version of yourself.

Because real influence doesn't come from what you say—it comes from who you are.

This is Anna, Thinking Out Loud

You're never fully dressed without a Smile

Attitude is Everything

Your mindset shapes your reality. The way you approach life's challenges, opportunities, and setbacks determines your success and fulfilment. Elevate your attitude, and everything else will follow.

√ **Stay Positive** – Your thoughts create your reality. Keep them optimistic.

√ **Stay Focused** – Distractions are everywhere; discipline keeps you on track.

√ **Refuse to be a Victim** – Take control of your narrative. Your past doesn't define you.

√ **Face Your Fears** – The things you fear most often hold the greatest rewards.

√ **Feed Your Soul** – Do what brings you joy, as long as it harms no one—including yourself.

√ **Find Passion in Your Work** – Love what you do, and showing up won't feel like a chore.

√ **Embrace Change** – Growth means evolving. Let your dreams shift with you.

√ **Change Your Environment** – Stuck in a rut? A simple change of scenery—like a park bench or a coffee shop—can spark new motivation.

√ **Delegate and Free Yourself** – You don't have to do it all alone. Share the load and make time for you.

√ **Think Like a Winner** – Positive thinkers create positive results.

√ **Own Your Individuality** – You're unique for a reason. Stand in your truth.

√ **Keep Growing** – Learn. Live. Love. Evolve.

√ **Invest in Yourself** – You are incredible—keep becoming even better!

Your attitude is your superpower. Cultivate it, and watch how your life transforms!

This is Anna, Thinking Out Loud!

Exploring Your Inner Landscape Exercise

Write down three beliefs that you hold about yourself which could be limiting your confidence.

1. _____
2. _____
3. _____

Now change these for three beliefs you would rather have.

1. _____
2. _____
3. _____

What would you have to do to make these beliefs come true?

1. _____
2. _____
3. _____
4. _____
5. _____
6. _____

This is Anna, Thinking Out Loud!

Fear is a liar
It helps activate the
enemy...
Be strong, be brave
& watch fear release
It's hold on you.....

This is Anna, Thinking Out Loud!

Breaking the Cycle: It Stops with You

Let's be real—some of the things we carry were never ours to begin with.

They were handed down, quietly or chaotically, from people who didn't know any better. Pain gets passed on when it's never processed. Silence becomes a language. Shame becomes a legacy. And before we know it, we're reacting to life with emotions and patterns that belong to someone else's story.

But here's the truth no one may have told you:

You are allowed to put it down.

You do not have to inherit their wounds.

You do not have to continue their silence.

You do not have to wear their mistakes like your own skin.

Healing is not betrayal.

Choosing peace is not disloyalty.

It's not your job to carry it all—but it can be your choice to transform it.

Reflecting on the Chain

Sometimes it takes a moment of pause to see the link you've become in a long, heavy chain. Maybe it's the way you shut down when things get tough, because that's how conflict was handled in your house. Maybe it's the constant apologising, the self-doubt, the perfectionism, the fear of being "too much"—things you picked up while growing up in someone else's storm.

And yet, here we are—waking up. Asking questions. Choosing awareness over autopilot. That's how the chain begins to loosen.

Because breaking the cycle isn't always loud. Sometimes it's a whisper that says,

"This pattern stops with me."

Sometimes it's saying no when you were taught to say yes.

Sometimes it's setting a boundary, even if your voice shakes.

Sometimes it's choosing love—real love—over the version of love you were modelled, the one laced with conditions.

You don't owe the past your future.

And your healing isn't just for you—it ripples forward, softening the road for those who come after you.

Breaking the Cycle: It Stops with You – Practical Exercises

Reflection: Who Gave You What?

Sit with this for a moment.

- What patterns or beliefs have been passed down through your family?

- What did you learn—directly or indirectly—about love, anger, vulnerability, and self-worth?
- Who taught you how to trust? Who taught you how to shut down?

You don't need to blame to be aware. This isn't about pointing fingers. It's about lifting the veil and seeing clearly, because clarity is the beginning of change.

If it feels heavy, that's okay. You're not meant to figure it all out in one sitting. You're simply giving yourself permission to see.

Exercise 1: The Line Stops Here

Take a blank page. Draw a vertical line down the middle.

Title one side: "What I Inherited"

Title the other side: "What I Intend to Pass On"

On the left side, list the emotional habits, messages, and patterns that were handed to you — even the ones that came wrapped in love.

On the right side, write what you are choosing instead. More honesty? Boundaries? Emotional availability? Gentleness? Confidence?

This is your declaration. Your reset.

Your refusal to let what broke them break you too.

Reflection: You Don't Owe Pain Your Loyalty

Sometimes we stay in cycles out of guilt. We think that healing means turning our backs on the people who raised us. But here's the truth: loving your family and friends doesn't mean becoming them.

Breaking the cycle is an act of love—for your past, your present, and everyone who comes after you.

You can love people and still say,

"This part ends with me."

Exercise 2: Write a Letter to the Cycle

This is for your eyes only.

Write a letter addressed to the pain, the silence, the dysfunction — whatever pattern you're ready to release. Name it. Talk to it. Let it know what it did, how it made you feel, what it taught you, and why you're choosing to let it go now.

You can end your letter however you want. Here's one way:

"I see what you were. I see where you came from. And I see how far I've come.

I'm not angry anymore—but I'm also not yours to control.

I'm done carrying what was never mine.

I choose freedom. I choose healing.

It stops with me."

Now tear it up. Burn it safely. Or keep it as a reminder that you are not broken—you're becoming.

Final Words: You Are the Shift

If no one has told you lately—I will.

You are powerful.

You are not what happened to you.

You are what you decide to do with it.

It doesn't matter who came before you.

You are the one who is changing the narrative.

You are the one who is showing what's possible.

You are the shift your lineage has been waiting for.

And trust me—that's no small thing.

This is Anna, Thinking Out Loud

The Cycle Ends Here

I release what was never mine to carry,

I let go of what was taught in pain.

I choose peace over echoes of fury,

And break free from the past's cruel chain.

No more silence, no more shame,

I walk forward, not the same.

I stand tall, I stand strong,

I am whole, and I belong.

This is my truth, this is my prayer—

I am free. I am whole. I am here!

This is Anna, Thinking Out Loud

You are reclaiming strength and you're doing it with truth, grace and fire.

This is Anna, Thinking Out Loud!

How to Recognise a Narcissistic Partner

Being in a relationship with a narcissist can be emotionally exhausting and damaging. Narcissists manipulate, control, and diminish their partners to maintain dominance. Recognising the signs early and taking steps to protect yourself is crucial for your mental and emotional well-being.

If you're constantly feeling drained, confused, or devalued in your relationship, you might be dealing with a narcissistic partner. Here are some common red flags:

Lack of Empathy

They disregard your feelings, struggles, and emotions. They may act indifferent to your pain and fail to acknowledge your emotional needs.

Excessive Need for Admiration

They constantly seek praise, attention and validation, making you feel like you're never doing enough to satisfy them.

Manipulation & Gaslighting

They twist the truth, make you doubt your own reality, and shift blame to avoid accountability. You may find yourself questioning your memory or perception of events.

Control & Domination

They dictate your choices, from how you dress to who you spend time with, often isolating you from friends and family.

Blame-Shifting

They never take responsibility for their actions. Everything is always your fault, and they make you feel guilty for their shortcomings.

Entitlement

They believe they deserve special treatment without giving anything in return. They expect unwavering devotion without reciprocating effort or kindness.

Emotional Rollercoaster

They alternate between love-bombing (excessive affection, gifts, promises) and devaluation (criticism, withdrawal, ignoring you), leaving you in a constant state of emotional turmoil.

Verbal & Emotional manipulation

They may insult, belittle, or intimidate you to maintain control over the relationship.

Narcissistic relationships drain you of your self-worth, confidence, and peace. It's crucial to recognise when you're in one and take steps to protect yourself.

This is Anna, Thinking Out Loud!

How to Protect Yourself from a Narcissist & Exit Safely

If you've identified narcissistic traits in your partner, it's essential to take steps to safeguard your mental, emotional, and even physical well-being. Here's how:

1. Trust Your Instincts

If something feels off, it probably is. Don't dismiss your gut feelings. You are not overreacting or imagining things.

2. Set Boundaries

Narcissists hate boundaries. Be clear about what you will and won't tolerate. Stand firm in your limits, even if they try to push back.

3. Limit Emotional Reactions

Narcissists thrive on emotional responses. Stay calm and disengage instead of reacting to their provocations.

4. Seek Support

Confide in trusted friends, family, or a therapist. A strong support system can provide clarity and encouragement.

5. Don't Engage in Power Struggles

Arguing with a narcissist is often pointless. They twist narratives to serve their ego. Instead, focus on protecting your peace.

6. Plan Your Exit

If you decide to leave, do so strategically. Have a financial and emotional plan in place, especially if they control money or resources.

7. Go 'No Contact'

If possible, cut off all communication. If you must stay in touch (co-parenting, shared responsibilities), keep interactions minimal and strictly factual.

8. Seek Professional Help

A therapist experienced in narcissistic abuse can provide strategies for healing and moving forward. Therapy can help rebuild your self-esteem and break free from toxic patterns.

9. Remember: It's Not Your Fault

You didn't cause their behaviour, and you don't have to endure it. Prioritise your well-being over their demands.

Final Thoughts

You deserve the love that nurtures, not love that destroys. Surround yourself with people who uplift, support, and appreciate you for who you are. The first step toward healing is realising your worth—never settle for less.

This is Anna, Thinking Out Loud!

If you don't have the capacity to love her right, then step aside & stop blocking her blessings for the one she deserves...

This is Anna, Thinking Out Loud!

Awakening Your Authenticity

What are three positive and helpful activities that you will commit to doing in the next week or so?

1._____

2._____

3. _____

Revisit this area to confirm if you were able to carry out your commitments.

Did anything embolden you?

_____

_____

_____

Did anything deter or hinder you?

_____

_____

_____

Now take a deep breath and send compassion and care to yourself.

This is Anna, Thinking Out Loud!

What is a Personal Boundary & Why Boundaries Matter

A line you draw to protect all or part of your life from being controlled, manipulated, fixed, misunderstood, abused, discounted or demeaned.

Personal boundaries protect you from manipulation and exploitation. Think of them as an investment in yourself—your knowledge, body, skills, abilities, purpose, and well-being. When you set and enforce boundaries, you safeguard your personal wealth.

1. Boundaries Define Who You Are

Clear boundaries give you confidence, helping others understand what you stand for and what to expect from you. This, in turn, attracts positive relationships and opportunities that align with your values.

2. Boundaries Affirm Your Worth

When you set boundaries, you reinforce your sense of identity. They serve as a declaration of who you are, ensuring that you are seen, heard, and taken seriously.

3. Boundaries Protect You from Harm

Without boundaries, you become vulnerable to unhealthy influences—people, habits, and situations that drain or diminish you. Saying "no" to what doesn't serve you and "yes" to what does is an act of self-respect.

4. Boundaries Speak for You

Your energy and presence often communicate your boundaries before you even say a word. Those who respect them will naturally gravitate toward you, while those who seek to overstep will be deterred.

5. Boundaries Foster Healthy Relationships

People admire those who set clear boundaries because it signals self-awareness and self-respect. In turn, they are more likely to respect your boundaries and establish their own.

6. Boundaries Strengthen Your Resilience

Criticism and pushback are inevitable, but strong boundaries help you stand firm. They protect your mental and emotional well-being, allowing you to navigate challenges without compromising your values.

Boundaries are not barriers—they are the foundation of self-respect, healthy relationships, and personal freedom. The better you define them, the more empowered you become.

Housekeeping

Keep checking in regularly with your boundaries. What has changed, what alterations will you need to make, what will you need to add…

Life speedily changes & there will be more commotion, more challenges, more competition, more experiences and more relationships, both personal & professional.

So my question is - What will you let in? Keep out? Give? Receive? Whatever it is, check to make sure that it does not adversely infringe on the boundaries you have set for yourself.

This is Anna, Thinking Out Loud!

Make love to her
mind, before her
body & then her
Soul will be
nourished...

This is Anna, Thinking Out Loud!

Strong but Tired... It's Time to Rest

To those who carry the weight of strength for everyone and every day but find themselves exhausted—this is for you.

You have permission to rest.

You are not responsible for fixing everything, every single day—not for others, and not even for yourself. Some things will work themselves out in time. You don't always have to be the problem-solver, the caretaker, or the one who holds everything together.

It's beautiful to support others, to bring joy, and to be the one people rely on. But remember—you don't have to pour from an empty cup. Let others take responsibility for themselves. It's okay to step back, to allow space, and to trust that life will keep moving even when you take a break.

Breathe. Pause. Recharge.

Give yourself permission to just be. Whatever brings you joy—do it. And do it fully, without guilt. Love yourself enough to rest, to nurture your mind and body, to prioritise your well-being.

Your strength is undeniable, but even the strongest need moments of stillness. Rest is not a weakness—it's the fuel that keeps your fire burning.

Take your moment. You deserve it.

Leonardo Da Vinci once said:

'Every now and then go away, have a little relaxation, for when you come back to your work, your judgement will be sure. Go some distance away because then the work appears smaller and more of it can be taken in at a glance, and a lack of harmony and proportion is more readily seen.'

This is Anna, Thinking Out Loud!

Practicing Self-Care Exercise. Uncover Your True Self

Make yourself a priority and take small steps to practice self-care and regain your well-being and stamina.

What self-care activities can you do daily, weekly, monthly?

_____

_____

_____

_____

_____

_____

_____

_____

Write down your commitment and bookmark it as a visible place to return to. Take a picture and save it on your phone, or post your commitments somewhere you will see it daily.

This is Anna, Thinking Out Loud!

Understanding Motivation & Turning It into Action

Motivation is the driving force behind everything we do. Understanding what fuels your motivation can help you create a clear and actionable path toward your goals. Here's how:

1. Identify Your Driving Force

We are motivated by:

A Want or a Need – What do you deeply desire? What is lacking in your life that you need to fulfil? Write down your top three needs or desires that currently drive you.

Perceptions of Pleasure & Pain – What brings you joy? What do you fear or want to avoid? Reflect on how you can use these forces to push yourself forward.

Hopes & Expectations – What future outcome do you expect? Do you believe in your ability to reach your goals? If not, what mindset shifts are needed?

2. Create a Goal-Oriented Plan

Now, turn your motivation into a structured plan:

Define Your Goal: Be specific. Instead of "I want to be healthier," say, "I will exercise for 30 minutes, five days a week."

Find Your Why: Ask yourself, Why do I want this? Tie it to your core motivations (needs, pleasure/pain, or hopes).

Set a Timeline: Without deadlines, motivation fades. Break your goal into smaller milestones and set a target date for each.

Identify Obstacles & Solutions: What might stop you? Plan ways to overcome setbacks before they happen.

Reward Progress: Celebrate small wins! This taps into the pleasure-driven aspect of motivation, keeping you excited and engaged.

3. Action Exercise: Motivation Map

Take a moment to complete this:

What is one goal I want to achieve?

_____
_____
_____
_____
_____
_____

Why do I want this? (What need, pleasure, or hope does it fulfil?)

_____
_____
_____
_____

_____

_____

What are three small actions I can take this week to move toward this goal?

How will I celebrate my progress?

_____
_____
_____
_____
_____
_____

By understanding what drives you and creating a structured plan, you transform motivation into momentum. Now, take the first step!

This is Anna, Thinking Out Loud!

Seeking Phronesis

The Greek term **phronesis,** often translated as "wisdom" in the New Testament, actually carries a deeper meaning—**practical wisdom**. This is illustrated in the parable: "He is like the wise man who built his house upon the rock." The message isn't just about intelligence but about using wisdom in **action**—laying a strong foundation for life that can withstand storms and challenges.

In this sense, **phronesis** is not just about knowing what is right but also applying that knowledge in a way that leads to stability, resilience and success.

For anyone on a journey of self-discovery and personal growth, seeking **practical wisdom** is essential. It's about learning not just from books or theory but from experience—your own and that of others.

This is why having a *"chosen person"*—a mentor, guide, or elder—can be life-changing. Ideally, this should be someone with:

Life experience – Someone who has navigated hardships and learned from them.

A strong moral and ethical compass – Someone whose wisdom is rooted in integrity.

The ability to offer practical solutions – Not just theoretical advice, but guidance you can act on.

By embracing **phronesis**, you take control of your growth, ensuring that the wisdom you acquire is not just knowledge but a tool for real change and healing. Practical wisdom isn't passive—it is the active force that builds a strong foundation, shaping the life you desire.

This is Anna, Thinking Out Loud!

Are You Caught in the Cycle of Self-Defeating Behaviours?

Do you ever feel like you're standing in your own way? Self-defeating behaviours are patterns that pull you away from the goals you've set, leaving you feeling drained, frustrated, and stuck. These habits can be subtle, yet they have a powerful impact on your confidence, relationships, and overall well-being.

Do Any of These Sound Familiar?

- **Defensiveness** – Reacting to feedback with resistance instead of openness.
- **Worrying** – Overthinking and doubting yourself at every turn.
- **Perfectionism** – Setting impossible standards, leading to frustration and burnout.
- **Isolation** – Withdrawing from others due to fear or insecurity.
- **Lack of Confidence** – Second-guessing your abilities and worth.
- **Procrastination** – Delaying important tasks out of fear of failure.

- **Escapism & Denial** – Avoiding reality instead of facing challenges head-on.

At some point, these behaviours may have served as coping mechanisms, but over time, they sabotage the very success and happiness you're trying to achieve.

The Connection Between Thoughts, Feelings, and Actions

Every aspect of our behaviour is linked—how we act, think, feel, and even sense the world around us. When we fall into self-defeating patterns, negativity feeds negativity. The key to breaking free? Learning how to recognise, express, and release the thoughts and emotions that fuel these behaviours.

Your Self-Image Shapes Your Life

Your self-image—the way you see yourself—is built on three key foundations:

1. **Self-Worth**– How much value do you place on yourself? How comfortable are you with who you are?

2. **Competence**– Do you believe in your ability to solve problems and achieve your goals? This is the foundation of confidence.

3. **Belonging**– Do you feel accepted and respected by those around you?

Your self-esteem is a reflection of these factors, shaped by your upbringing, life experiences, and environment. But the good news? You can rebuild and strengthen it, one step at a time.

The Power of Assertiveness

One of the most effective ways to overcome self-defeating behaviours is by developing **assertiveness**—the ability to express your needs, values, and boundaries with confidence while respecting others.

When you stand up for yourself, you take control of your life. You no longer allow yourself to be pressured, manipulated, or dismissed. Instead, you gain respect, build stronger relationships, and create a life that aligns with your true self.

It's Time to Take Charge

- Express your thoughts and feelings openly.
- Acknowledge and respect others' viewpoints without sacrificing your own.
- Say "yes" or "no" without guilt.
- Stop carrying responsibility for others' problems.

The way people treat you is a reflection of what you allow. When you assert yourself, you teach others how to respect you. Confidence isn't arrogance—it's knowing your worth without needing validation.

Break free from self-defeating behaviours and step into the life you deserve. It starts with you.

This is Anna, Thinking Out Loud!

You Again…

Yes, you. The only person standing between you and your potential is **You**. But here's the truth—within you already lies something extraordinary: **Greatness.**

I'm here to help you uncover it.

Emotions—your **passions, reactions, excitements, and sensations** — are not just fleeting feelings; they shape your choices, your relationships, and your very existence. The key is not to suppress them but to **understand, regulate, and express them with purpose**.

When you truly recognise what you're feeling and why, you gain control over your inner world. And when you master your emotions, you also begin to understand the emotions of others—allowing you to navigate life with clarity, confidence, and grace.

This journey is about **you**—becoming the person you were always meant to be. The time to start is right now.

What truly holds you back? Is it fear? Doubt? The weight of past experiences?

If you pause and reflect, what are the invisible barriers that keep you from moving forward? Are they external circumstances, or do they come from within?

Could it be that the greatest obstacle isn't the world around you, but the thoughts and beliefs you carry?

Take a moment—what are the things that hamper you? List them. See them clearly.

_____

_____

_____

_____

_____

_____

Now ask yourself: **Are they as immovable as they seem?**

This is Anna, Thinking Out Loud!

Your Locus of Evaluation

Write down three beliefs that you hold about yourself which could be limiting your confidence and change these for three beliefs you would rather have.

Limiting Belief   New Positive Belief

_____   _____
_____   _____
_____   _____
_____   _____
_____   _____

What would you have to do to make these beliefs come true?

_____
_____
_____

Write down the date that you work on each belief in order to monitor your progress of success from start to finish.

Date: _____
Date: _____
Date: _____
Date: _____

This is Anna, Thinking Out Loud!

The drama, the conflict, the insecurities, the negative thoughts is all your own doing. Take responsibility for yourself & watch the game change!

This is Anna, Thinking Out Loud!

Why Don't We Listen?

We see the red flags. We feel the unease. Our instincts whisper, our past experiences resurface, and yet—**we ignore the warning signs.**

Why do we do this? Why do we silence the very signals meant to protect us?

Too often, people find themselves in situations where they are mistreated, manipulated, or even abused—sometimes subtly, sometimes blatantly. But instead of confronting the truth, we engage in what is called the **"Ostrich Syndrome"**—burying our heads in the sand to avoid acknowledging what we already know deep down.

We dismiss small signs of control. We excuse behaviours that make us uncomfortable. We convince ourselves, *"It's not a big deal."* But here's the truth: **It is a big deal.** And if left unchallenged, it will only grow into something bigger. **Your Instincts Are There for a Reason!**

Think about this: Have you ever crossed the street because someone walking toward you or behind you felt *off*? That gut feeling—that prefrontal warning system—wasn't random. It was your body protecting you, urging you to take action for your own peace of mind and safety.

If we trust our instincts in everyday situations—on the street, in a supermarket, in a parking area—why don't we trust them in our personal and intimate relationships?

Start Listening. Start Protecting Yourself.

It's time to stop ignoring the signs. Pay attention to:

- Words spoken—and unspoken.
- Actions and reactions.
- How someone makes you feel—consistently.

Your safety, your well-being, and your peace of mind **matter.** Trust yourself. Listen to yourself. And most importantly—**act on what you hear.**

This is Anna, Thinking Out Loud!

When Will You Finally Recognise Your Own Worth?

When will you wake up and see the value in yourself—the respect, love, and care you truly deserve?

Why do you continue to stay in situations that **diminish you**, that **fail to uplift you**, that **take from you without giving back**?

- When your partner belittles and criticises you, that is not love.
- When they seek intimacy but refuse to hold you, kiss you, or cherish you before, during, and after, that is not love.
- When they let you carry the weight—literally and emotionally—while benefiting from your efforts, that is not love.
- When they mock your appearance, your style, or your body, while ignoring their own flaws, that is not love.
- When they betray your trust without remorse and still demand your loyalty, that is not love.
- When they never make time to connect, unwind, or simply *be* with you, that is not love.

100

- When they hurt you with words, actions, or silence and refuse to acknowledge their wrongs, that is not love.
- When they keep you waiting for a commitment that never comes, yet expect you to give them everything as if it already has—that is **not** love.

This is what you have accepted. This is what you have allowed. And the pain, the emptiness, the frustration—it will remain **until you decide that you deserve better.**

You will never experience true peace, true joy, or true fulfilment **until you choose to honour yourself.**

So, I ask you again—**when will you wake up and recognise your own significance?**

This is Anna, Thinking Out Loud!

The Reflection That Truly Matters, Man in the Mirror

Michael Jackson once sang, *"I'm talking to the man in the mirror, I'm asking him to change his ways."* Those words hold immense power—an urgent call to self-reflection and transformation.

But what if, when we looked in the mirror, we saw more than just our physical reflection? What if we truly saw the **content of our character**? Would we still focus on fine lines and blemishes, or would we begin to **nurture our spirit, refine our actions, and correct our missteps**?

Perhaps then, instead of simply applying more moisturiser to the skin, we would start applying **kindness, integrity, and growth** to our souls. Instead of obsessing over surface-level flaws, we would focus on becoming the person the Universe knows we are capable of being.

At the end of the day, it is not the perfection of your face but the **purity of your heart** that truly matters. And that is the reflection that the Universe sees.

This is Anna, Thinking Out Loud!

Searching for Peace

We can endure anything when we have the right tools and the strength to tap into our inner power. **Peace is not found in the absence of hardship, but in our ability to rise above it.**

Everyone seeks happiness. No one welcomes pain. Yet, life reminds us time and time again—growth is born from struggle, and wisdom is carved from experience.

If you want a rainbow, you must first accept the storm. There is no sun without rain, no true joy without moments of reflection, no transformation without the renewal of the spirit. Every challenge you face is not meant to break you but to **awaken you**—to show you the resilience, courage, and limitless strength that already exists within you.

You are not powerless. You hold within you the ability to heal, to rise, and to move forward, no matter how difficult the journey may seem. Peace is not something to be found—it is something to be **created, cultivated, and claimed** within yourself.

Take life one day at a time. Trust the process. You are stronger than you know.

This is Anna, Thinking Out Loud!

Who said you can't? Of course you can Sis

Fixed Mindset -vs- Growth Mindset:

Are You Settling or Thriving?

A **fixed mindset** might convince you that what's available in this world is as good as it gets—that you have to accept certain flaws or risk being alone. You may tell yourself, *"There isn't much better out there. If I don't accept these imperfections, I'll end up alone."*

You might even believe that your ideal partner—someone who truly aligns with your values—simply doesn't exist, no matter what you do.

But here's the real question:

Are you consciously choosing what you accept in your life, or are you settling by default?

And what can you do differently to create meaningful change in this area?

The Standard You Deserve

When considering a partner, ask yourself:

√ Does he or she align with your self-worth?

√ Does he or she share your drive, determination, and vision for the future?

√ Does he or she show respect—holding doors, pulling out chairs, being mindful of his or her language around you?

√ Is he or she consistent in their actions—showing up, calling, and staying present in your life?

√ Do his or her words uplift, support and empower you?

√ Does he or she spend meaningful, constructive time with the children?

√ Does he or she attend parent-teacher meetings?

√ Has he made an effort to integrate his kids into your shared life and routines?

√ Is he financially responsible—earning an income, paying taxes, and building stability?

√ Does he have a strong work ethic—reliable, punctual, and dependable?

√ Is he steadfast and strong—wise, forward-thinking, and full of purpose?

√ Does he or she make you feel valued in the time they spend with you?

√ Does he or she genuinely try to meet your wants, needs and desires?

√ Is your time together exciting, fun, and emotionally intimate?

√ When he or she makes mistakes, do they take accountability and strive to do better?

√ Is he or she open to trying new things and growing with you?

Growth Mindset: The Power of Believing You Deserve More

A **growth mindset** reminds you that you don't have to settle. It empowers you to focus on the love, respect, and joy you truly ask for. You don't lower your standards out of fear—you uphold them because you believe in yourself. And because you believe in yourself, you know that love, respect, and fulfilment are not just possible—they are indeed your standard.

So now, I ask you:

How are you celebrating what you've manifested and welcomed into your life?

And what can you do additionally to keep growing in this area?

This is Anna, Thinking Out Loud!

Mama Used to Say...

Mama had a way of saying things that, as children, made absolutely no sense to us—at least not at the time. One of her favourites, spoken in her thick Caribbean accent, was:

"Yuh nah reach anywhere unless yuh stop carry water inna basket."

My siblings and I would steal glances at each other, barely suppressing our eye-rolls, careful not to let Mama catch us. To us, it was just another one of her peculiar sayings, words that seemed to belong to another time, another world.

It wasn't until years later—after diving into the wisdom of great thinkers, of a lived experience, and studying the works of psychologists—that I finally understood just how profound her words really were. Her message echoed the sentiment of Albert Einstein's famous quote:

"Insanity is doing the same thing over and over again and expecting different results."

For those who still might not see where I'm going with this, let me break it down. A **basket** is a container woven from materials like cane, wire, or wood splints. But here's the thing—it's **porous**. Water will always seep through. So, if you keep trying to carry water in the basket, no matter how many times you try, the result will always be the same: **an empty basket** at the end of your journey.

In other words:

"If you always do what you have always done, then you will always get what you always got."

(A sentiment often attributed to Henry Ford.)

It turns out, Mama, Einstein, and Ford were speaking the same truth—each in their own way. **Genius recognises genius, after all.**

And maybe, just maybe, Mama knew **exactly** what she needed to say in a way that would be long-lasting in the memories of her Loved Ones.

My Mama, she was likkle but she was Tallawah!

(The phrase is often used to highlight that whilst small in stature, she possesses great strength in character, determination, talent and ability. It serves as a reminder of true strength).

This is Anna, Thinking Out Loud!

Moving Forward with Strength: Reclaiming Yourself After a Breakup

Ending a relationship, no matter the circumstances, can be a deeply emotional experience. It's natural to reflect on both the mistakes and the beautiful moments. However, dwelling too long in the past can keep you from embracing your future.

- Acknowledge both the good and the bad, but don't let them define you.
- The relationship has ended, and now is the time to reclaim your power and step into a new chapter with confidence.

Own Your Power

Feeling like a victim can make you believe that life is happening *to* you rather than *for* you. But here's the truth: you have the ability to shape your future.

- You have complete control over how you respond to this moment.
- You always have a choice in how you process and move forward.

- Healing isn't instant, but shifting your mindset will bring you clarity and joy.

Release the Past, Embrace the Present

Ruminating over what went wrong keeps you stuck. To truly move on, you must free yourself from the weight of resentment and regret.

- Reliving past grievances keeps you anchored in negativity.
- The energy you spend resenting an ex could be used to build a better future for yourself.
- Letting go isn't just about them—it's about liberating yourself from emotional baggage.

Reconnect with Life

Healing takes time, but isolating yourself prolongs the pain. Instead, choose to re-engage with the world.

- Surround yourself with supportive friends and uplifting activities.
- Prioritise joy—whether that's through hobbies, travel, or self-care.
- If you're open to dating, consider "Recreational Dating"—meeting new people without pressure or expectations. Be upfront about where you stand and focus on enjoying yourself.

Be Intentional About Your Next Chapter

It might be tempting to fill the void with someone new, but rushing into another relationship before you're ready can lead to repeating past patterns.

- Take time to understand what *you* need to be happy and fulfilled.
- Focus on becoming your best self before seeking a new partner.
- When you're whole on your own, you'll attract a relationship that truly complements you.

Embrace Your Future With Confidence

You are not defined by a failed relationship. You are resilient, capable, and deserving of happiness. This ending is not a loss—it's an opportunity for growth, self-discovery, and an even brighter future ahead. Step forward courageously—you've got this.

"Be patient and tough, one day this pain will be useful to you."

—*Ovid*

This is Anna, Thinking Out Loud!

Embracing Life's Ups and Downs with Strength

Life is a journey of highs and lows, and at times, it can feel like we're drifting—searching for something missing, whether it's peace, joy, laughter, or companionship. These moments of uncertainty push us to reflect, explore, and take action to create a more fulfilling life.

- It's natural to seek inspiration from others, but remember, you are your greatest teacher.
- Growth comes from within—while people, books, and guidance can offer insights, only *you* can put the pieces of your life's puzzle together.
- Trust your journey. With patience and faith, you *will* find clarity, purpose, and fulfilment.

Life isn't about having everything figured out at once—it's about embracing the process, trusting yourself, and knowing that every challenge brings you closer to becoming the best version of yourself.

Take the first step in faith,

You don't have to see the entire staircase…

Just take the first step!

—*Dr Martin Luther King*

What steps will you be taking going forward? List them here:

_____
_____
_____
_____
_____
_____
_____
_____

This is Anna, Thinking Out Loud!

Her expectations changed, She focused on herself & She started to Win....

This is Anna, Thinking Out Loud!

Shifting Focus: Seeing the Green Flags in Relationships

When we move on from past relationships and step into new ones, we often become hyper-aware of red flags. While being cautious is important, this focus can sometimes make us overlook the *green flags*—the signs of a healthy, supportive, and fulfilling relationship.

Why We Overlook Green Flags

- Past Hurt Shapes Our Perspective – Previous heartbreaks can make us more alert to warning signs, sometimes to the point where we expect things to go wrong.
- Confirmation Bias – When we believe relationships are bound to fail, we unconsciously look for proof that supports this belief while ignoring signs of positivity.
- Self-Protection Mode – Guarding ourselves against pain is natural, but true emotional growth comes from recognising when it's safe to be open again.

The Importance of Noting Green Flags

Red flags help us avoid unhealthy relationships, but green flags help us recognise and appreciate a *healthy* one. Noting green flags allows us to:

- Build trust based on real actions rather than fear.
- Enjoy the relationship rather than analyse it for faults.
- Strengthen emotional connection by valuing positive traits in our partner.

How to Recognise Green Flags in a Relationship

1. Emotional Availability – Your partner communicates openly and makes space for your feelings.
2. Consistency in Actions – They show up for you in words *and* actions, proving their reliability.
3. Respect for Boundaries – They honour your needs and don't pressure you into anything uncomfortable.
4. Supportive and Encouraging – They celebrate your successes and encourage your growth.
5. Conflict is Handled Maturely – Disagreements are resolved with respect rather than blame or manipulation.
6. Mutual Effort – They invest time and energy into making the relationship work, just as you do.

Shifting Your Mindset: How to Focus on Green Flags

- Balance Your Perspective – If you're quick to notice red flags, challenge yourself to find green flags too.
- Keep a Relationship Journal – Write down positive moments and patterns of kindness and support.
- Reflect on Your Own Growth – Ask yourself: *Am I allowing myself to see the good, or am I bracing for the worst?*
- Talk to Trusted Friends – Sometimes, an outside perspective can help highlight the positives we may overlook.
- Practice Gratitude – Appreciating what's going *right* in your relationship helps shift your focus from fear to fulfilment.

Concluding Thoughts

While it's important to remain aware of red flags, don't let fear prevent you from embracing a healthy, loving relationship. Noticing green flags allows you to build trust, deepen connections, and create a fulfilling partnership.

Love should be about growth and joy, not just avoiding pain. Be open to the good—it's there, waiting to be seen.

Talking to Trusted Friends—Trust Yourself First

Having a trusted friend's perspective can be incredibly valuable when navigating a new relationship. They can help highlight the positive qualities you might be overlooking and provide reassurance when doubts creep in. However, it's important to remember that your friends view relationships through their own personal lens, shaped by their past experiences, biases, and sometimes even their own fears or disappointments.

While advice from loved ones can be insightful, relying on it too much can cloud your judgment. If a friend has been hurt before, they may unconsciously project their own negative experiences onto your situation, warning you of dangers that may not actually exist. Instead of offering an objective viewpoint, they may reinforce your own fears rather than helping you see the situation clearly.

So, how do you strike a healthy balance?

- **Seek input, but don't let it override your intuition.** Listen to different perspectives, but always check in with yourself. How do *you* feel? What do *you* see?
- **Choose your confidants wisely.** Some friends give thoughtful, unbiased advice, while others react from their own emotional history. Be selective about who you turn to.
- **Limit overanalysing with friends.** Constantly discussing every detail of your relationship can keep you in a cycle of doubt and confusion. Sometimes, you just need to experience the relationship without external noise.

- **Keep space for your own perspective.** Journaling, meditation, or simply spending quiet time reflecting on your emotions can help you form your own conclusions rather than relying solely on outside opinions.

At the end of the day, you are the one in the relationship. You are the one who experiences the green flags firsthand. Trust yourself enough to recognise them.

This is Anna, Thinking Out Loud!

Why Coping with Change Isn't Always Easy

Coping with change means navigating transitions—whether that's a shift in how we think or feel about ourselves, others, or a situation, or a more tangible move from one stage of life to another. Change can mean stepping into a new role, leaving something (or someone) behind, or confronting unfamiliar circumstances. And while change is a natural part of life, it doesn't always feel natural when we're going through it.

Each of us has a different capacity for handling change, but one thing is common: change—whether welcome or unwelcome—often brings resistance. Even positive changes can stir up discomfort because they disrupt our sense of normal.

Our past experiences with change also play a big part in how we respond to it now. We tend to carry the emotional memory of those experiences with us, sometimes more vividly than the events themselves.

How we cope with change depends on several key factors:

- How much control or choice we feel we have in the situation

- Whether we can respond in our own way, with autonomy and personal responsibility

To really understand why change feels so hard, we have to look at how the human mind works. Our brains are wired to seek safety in stability and predictability. When that's disrupted, it sends a signal that something might be wrong. This triggers a stress response—commonly known as "fight or flight"—and creates feelings of anxiety, fear, or confusion.

In response, the brain quickly starts evaluating the risks and potential rewards of the situation. Our reactions—hesitation, withdrawal, or even excitement—are shaped by this internal calculation.

So while change is part of growth, it often asks us to let go of the familiar—and that's never easy. But by understanding how our minds work and what influences our reactions, we can start to navigate change with more awareness and compassion for ourselves.

This is Anna, Thinking Out Loud!

Appease Yourself Sis

When you're struggling with life's challenges, remember—you're not alone. You are not the first to face difficulties, make mistakes, or have flaws. That's what makes you human. Be mindful not to believe every thought that crosses your mind. Sometimes, your mind can deceive you, making mountains out of molehills. The key is self-compassion.

Remember my acronym: CHILL...

Choose

Holistic

Invaluable

Life

Lessons

Take a walk in nature, feel the earth beneath your feet, and breathe in fresh air. Engage in a hobby that brings you pleasure. Listen to uplifting podcasts, play soothing music, and surround yourself with empathetic people. Stay hydrated, volunteer at a pet shop, try pottery, travel somewhere new, share laughter over coffee, learn to meditate, smile at a stranger and watch the kindness ripple back. Express gratitude for life's little blessings. Apologise when necessary. Embrace learning.

In other words—**Choose Holistic Invaluable Life Lessons. Just CHILL.**

This is Anna, Thinking Out Loud!

Are You Bringing Open Communication To Your Relationship

When meeting someone for the first time, it's natural to put your best foot forward. But beyond first impressions, **true connection requires authenticity and open communication**. Relationships thrive when expectations, needs, and responsibilities are discussed with honesty, clarity, and maturity.

One way to understand and improve communication is through **Transactional Analysis (TA),** a method developed by psychiatrist **Eric Berne (1910-1970)**. TA helps us recognise our communication patterns, increase self-awareness, and build stronger relationships. Berne believed that verbal communication is at the heart of human connection and I completely agree. When one person speaks (the **transactional stimulus**), the other responds (the**transactional response**). By understanding these exchanges, we can become more intentional in how we interact.

But how do we ensure our responses come from a place of emotional balance? This is where **self-awareness of personality and ego states** plays a crucial role.

Berne's **Transactional Analysis** builds on this by identifying three **ego states** that influence communication:

1. **The Parent State**– The voice of authority, often nurturing but sometimes critical.
2. **The Child State**– Emotional and instinctive, reacting with spontaneity or defiance.
3. **The Adult State**– Logical and balanced, focused on problem-solving and understanding.

In healthy relationships, communication flourishes when both partners **engage from the Adult state**, responding rather than reacting. Recognising when we are slipping into a **critical Parent mode** or an **impulsive Child state** can help prevent misunderstandings and conflict.

Applying Open Communication to Your Relationship

So, how can you bring open, intentional communication into your relationship?

Be mindful of your ego states—respond from your Adult state, not from impulse or authority.

Listen actively—communication is not just about speaking, but truly hearing your partner.

Clarify expectations—don't assume; discuss needs, boundaries, and goals.

Be honest yet kind—truth without empathy can be harsh; empathy without truth can be misleading.

Encourage dialogue, not monologue—real connection is a two-way street.

There's so much more to explore when it comes to how we communicate. At its core, **communication isn't just important—it's truly everything**. Be clear and kind. The way we express ourselves, listen, and interpret interactions determines the health of our relationships. Recognising how we interact with others—through Transactional Analysis, self-awareness, and honest dialogue and being conscious of your ego states, we can create deeper, more fulfilling connections.

So ask yourself: **Are you bringing open communication to your relationship?**

This is Anna, Thinking Out Loud!

Wife Material?

A man knows the worth of a good woman. He recognises when he has someone faithful, supportive, and nurturing by his side. He feels it in the way she loves him, cares for him, brings joy into his life, and helps him grow in ways he never could on his own. When I say *elevate*, I mean she brings him comfort, peace, and a sense of mental and emotional well-being.

But here's the question: **Does he honour you the way you honour him?**

You share children together. They carry his last name. And yet, he hasn't given you the honour of making You his wife. Meanwhile, you're the mother, the homemaker, the nurse, the counsellor, the teacher, the cook, the cleaner, the maid, and the assistant—on top of catering to his needs when he gets home.

If you desire marriage but he refuses to commit, ask yourself: **Why are you giving him everything that comes with the behaviour of a wife when he won't make you one?**

Stop pouring your energy, devotion, and love into a man who won't *fully* claim you. His mother gave birth to him—so if he refuses to step up and honour you the way you deserve, send him back home to her.

A man who truly values you will not hesitate to give you the same commitment and security that you've given him.

You may not agree with me, but

I'm just…. Thinking Out Loud

The Truth About Compromise: Are You Settling or Finding Balance?

We all know what compromise ***should*** mean—a fair agreement where both sides make concessions to reach a mutually beneficial outcome. But in reality, for many people, compromise in relationships often feels more like surrender—an acceptance of standards far lower than what they truly deserve.

Through countless conversations in both personal and professional settings, I've noticed a recurring theme: individuals often feel that compromise isn't about fairness, but about sacrificing their needs to maintain peace. Whether it's with a spouse, a colleague, a brother, or a friend, the pattern is the same—choosing the lesser of two evils rather than getting an outcome that genuinely respects both parties.

Take this example: A woman asks that her partner's friends not smoke inside their new home, especially since her young nephews are staying over. His "compromise." His friends can still smoke inside, but *he'll empty the ashtrays.* She's left with nothing but the illusion of a compromise—she still gets the very outcome she didn't want, minus the chore of cleaning up after. This isn't a balanced agreement; it's an outright dismissal of her concerns.

So, how do you shift from settling to **true** compromise?

The first step is recognising that real compromise isn't about diminishing your needs—it's about both parties adjusting in a way that respects each other. Many people, especially those with anxiety or a deep fear of conflict, avoid standing their ground because uncertainty feels overwhelming. But avoiding discomfort only leads to a life of shrinking choices and unspoken resentment.

Instead, practice stepping into those moments of unease. Voice your concerns, hold firm on your values, and recognise that a real compromise should never leave you feeling unheard. The more you push yourself to engage in uncomfortable discussions, the more you'll see that uncertainty isn't something to fear—it's something to navigate with confidence. You may not get all of what you want, but compromise must absolutely consist of getting *some* of what you need.

At the end of the day, compromise should never be about losing yourself—it should be about finding a way forward *together*.

This is Anna, Thinking Out Loud!

Exploring Histories Before We Date

If we truly grasped how much our past shapes our present, we'd start seeing ourselves—and our relationships—through an entirely new lens.

Our behaviours, reactions, and emotional patterns are deeply rooted in the experiences we've carried from childhood. The way we handle conflict, express love, and even perceive ourselves is often a reflection of what we learned early on. A child raised in a stable, nurturing environment typically grows into an emotionally balanced adult, while unresolved childhood wounds can manifest in self-doubt, fear of abandonment, or difficulty trusting others.

This is why understanding someone's past—without interrogation, but through genuine conversation—can be so revealing in relationships. How did they handle challenges as a child? Were their emotions validated or dismissed? These early experiences create a blueprint for how they'll navigate conflict and intimacy as an adult. When we recognise these patterns, we gain clarity, compassion, and the ability to respond with awareness rather than just react.

Intuition plays a key role in deciphering these unspoken influences. If we tune in, we can begin to see the motivations behind behaviours—both our own and those of others. The truth is, we're all shaped by our past. But by understanding its impact, we gain the power to break free from limiting patterns and create healthier, more fulfilling relationships.

This is Anna, Thinking Out Loud!

Did You Give Away Your Power....

If this is true, then it's time to reclaim your power and your life. Our minds have a way of only focusing on the hurt and pain caused in a relationship, whether it be *before*, *during* or *after* and this is called negative filtering.

When we give away our power, we allow our thoughts to be dominated by the pain, betrayal, or disappointment we've experienced. Negative filtering traps us in a cycle where we only see the hurtful aspects of a relationship, reinforcing feelings of helplessness and resentment. But reclaiming your power means shifting your perspective—it means acknowledging the pain without letting it define you. Instead of dwelling on what went wrong, recognise the lessons, the growth, and the buoyancy you've gained.

True empowerment comes when you realise that no person or situation has the authority to dictate your self-worth or happiness—only you do.

This is Anna, Thinking Out Loud!

To The Good Men

While I stand firm in empowering women, I also acknowledge that not all women uplift others with their behaviour and actions.

I can describe a case study where the female character consistently drained the energy from their relationships rather than adding to it and always led with their Histrionic Personality Disorder (HPD). This is a mental health condition characterised by excessive emotionality, attention-seeking behaviour, and a strong desire for approval. People with HPD often thrive on being the centre of attention and may use dramatic, seductive, or exaggerated behaviours to gain validation.

Aside from the described, there are other underserving women who act with entitlement, expecting luxury without effort, and their demands go like this:

"He better wine and dine me—but don't expect me to cook a damn thing."

"He better take me out every weekend."

"He better pay for my hair and nails."

"He better buy me the latest designer handbag."

"He better cut off his childhood friends and spend all his time with me."

"He better put me before his own family now that we're dating."

Yet these same women…

- Can't put together an edible meal.
- Have never paid for a date.
- Are petty and jealous at the mention of a female friend from childhood.
- Demand your time, yet won't have dinner ready after your long workday.
- Snoop through your phone and question why you spoke to your own mother for so long.
- Have your homeboys wondering, *"WTF, bro? when they see or feel her negativity and hate."*
- Lack the emotional maturity to explain or manage their behaviour.
- Show up looking half good, but bring nothing but drama.
- Manipulate your time, your peace, and your mind.
- Have no concept of *supporting their man's emotional and mental well-being.*

And let me tell you, *that kind of ugly runs deep.* Ugly mind. Ugly heart. Ugly Spirit and dark soul.

Gentlemen, Here's Some Wisdom:

Before making big decisions, consider allowing her the time and space to develop the life skills and emotional maturity she needs—don't rush her out of her parents' home to live together prematurely. Be mindful of your choices—always practice caution. Bringing a child into the world with someone unprepared could bring unnecessary hardship.

And to the Women:

If this sounds like you or resonates with you, take it as an opportunity for growth. Invest in your own development—work on yourself, for yourself, **and by yourself**.

To the Good Men:

If you encounter this kind of woman, take heed—step away. Your peace and future are worth far more than anything you might risk. Trust your instincts and move on swiftly.

Be patient until you walk into the arms of a worthy woman.

The good ones are out there, waiting for a good man.

Go forth, find your peace, and step into your happily ever after.

This is Anna, Thinking Out Loud!

If You're Not His Peace, Then Get Out Of His Way...

A man won't know **peace at home** if the woman he loves **feels like the enemy.** You **can't build a sanctuary** with someone who feels **like a threat** behind closed doors.

If you are not going to be his peace, then, in the words of rap artist Ludacris, "Move, b*tch, get out the way!"

Make room for his Cinderella or Sleeping Beauty—the woman who will honour him, uplift him, and align with his destiny. Because let's be real—your spite, pettiness, hatefulness, and negativity are taking up far too much space.

Everybody craves happiness; nobody seeks pain. So if you are not mature enough, kind enough, supportive enough, compassionate enough, helpful enough, or willing to compromise, then go back to your mama's house—and take your scornful, egregious, contemptuous, and Histrionic self with you.

Melanin Kings will rise when they are no longer shackled to a version of Mary M *before she met Jesus*—if you know, you know.

And to the Melanin Kings who have faced adversity, who were tricked and deceived by **deficient She-Devils** who gave nothing yet demanded everything—they hated the fact that you kept surviving. They despised that you kept winning. But why? Because they forgot one simple truth—

You are God-blessed. And who God blesses, no man can curse!

In Your Interest,

This is Anna, Thinking Out Loud!

It would have been remiss of me not to have at least one or two headings in support of the Fellas experience!

Get Out of Your Own Way, Sis

Sometimes, just sometimes, the biggest obstacle in a woman's life is herself.

Too often, we cause ourselves harm by refusing to confront our insecurities, ignoring our shortcomings, and holding on to bitterness like it's a badge of honour. We point fingers, cast blame, and grow frustrated with the world for not giving us what we feel we deserve — all the while never pausing to ask *why* we keep finding ourselves in the same painful patterns.

Here's the hard truth: negative thinking breeds negative outcomes. When we operate from a place of unhealed wounds and fear, we end up creating the very situations we dread. It's a self-fulfilling prophecy. **But the beautiful thing is — it doesn't have to stay that way.**

Growth starts with accountability. Real, uncomfortable, empowering accountability. The kind that requires honesty with ourselves. The kind that invites healing and transformation. If we truly want to be better, we must *do* better — not just in action, but in thought, intention, and energy.

Every woman has the power to shift her narrative. To stop surviving on blame and start thriving through ownership. To rise above the old stories and become the author of a new one.

Sis, get out of your own way—your higher self is waiting.

This is Anna, Thinking Out Loud!

Unshaken: The Morning She Stood in Her Power

Sometimes, life feels like an uphill battle, as if the odds are stacked against you, no matter how good of a person you are. Staying positive and overcoming challenges can feel exhausting.

One night, I went to bed weighed down by these thoughts on my mind. **But when I awoke, there was something new in my heart, something had shifted within me:**

People rarely see beyond my smile—they assume, misunderstand, and misrepresent me. **I am complex**, not because I intend to be, but because few know how to navigate **a soft heart wrapped in a warrior's soul**.

I was done feeling tired and drained.

I was done with understanding you before you understood me. I was done with accepting the things that did not serve my joy.

I was done with figuring out who is with me and who is against me.

Loyalty isn't just a concept; it is a way of living, and I will only surround myself with those who share the same mindset.

My mistakes are part of my growth, chapters in my story, not the title of my life **or** definition of my worth.

I rise. I shine. I soar.

That new dawn, that new day, that day I awoke brand new, I realised how necessary my own peace was—my own space, my own self-worth. **It was the day I chose to nourish my soul.**

I inhaled. I exhaled. **And suddenly, I felt free.**

Now, I remember the days that I prayed for the things I have right now and I am humble.

Now, I honour the sacred space within me where the Universe resides and I am grateful.

When will be your Phoenix moment? - the morning you choose to become the best version of Yourself?...

This is Anna, Thinking Out Loud!

The last time,
This time,
Next time...
I will always
unapologetically
choose me!

This is Anna, Thinking Out Loud!

Values truly Matter...

Your **values** are the core beliefs that shape your priorities and influence every area of your life—how you live, work, and interact with the world. They serve as your internal guide, helping you determine what truly matters and providing a sense of direction in decision-making.

When your goals and choices align with your values, life feels rich with purpose, fulfilment, and clarity. You experience a deep sense of satisfaction because your actions reflect what you genuinely believe in. However, when there's a disconnect between your values and the way you live, it can lead to frustration, discontent, and a feeling of being lost or unfulfilled. Over time, this misalignment can create a sense of hopelessness, making it difficult to find joy or meaning in your journey.

That's why making a **conscious effort** to define and understand your values is absolutely essential. They help you clarify what is truly important and serve as the foundation for making strong, decisive choices. They influence how you interact with the world, how you set and pursue your goals, and ultimately, how fulfilled you feel in life.

Your values may differ from those of others, and that's perfectly okay. **What matters most is that you honour what is important to you!** When you live in alignment with your values—especially those that define your sense of self and the way you cherish what is truly important—you cultivate a life of integrity, purpose, and lasting fulfilment.

Write down three of your core values:

1. _____
2. _____
3. _____

Now write down when and how you will implement them.

1. _____
2. _____
3. _____

Now, it's important to **regularly check in with your values**. As life evolves, your priorities and circumstances may shift, and it's essential to make sure you're still living in alignment with what truly matters to you. By reflecting on your values and adjusting your actions accordingly, you can stay on the path that leads to fulfillment, integrity, and personal growth.

This is Anna, Thinking Out Loud!

Relationships Fail Without Reciprocity

In every personal relationship—whether it's with family, friends, or romantic partners—**reciprocity** plays a vital role in maintaining balance, trust, and connection. Without reciprocity, relationships become one-sided, draining, and unsustainable. True connections thrive when there is **a mutual exchange of effort, support, and appreciation** between individuals.

Reciprocity shows that both parties value each other's time, energy, and emotions. It creates a foundation of **mutual respect**— when you see someone investing in you just as you invest in them, it solidifies the relationship and deepens the bond.

One-sided relationships—where one person is always giving while the other is constantly taking—breed **resentment and exhaustion**. When reciprocity is absent, the giver starts feeling unappreciated and drained, while the taker may become complacent and entitled. Healthy relationships require balance so that no one feels like they are carrying the entire emotional or physical load alone.

When reciprocity is present, a beautiful cycle of giving and receiving naturally forms. Instead of keeping track of who did what, both people contribute **out of love, care, and appreciation**, knowing that their efforts will be met with the same energy. This leads to healthier and happier relationships built on generosity rather than obligation.

Reciprocity is not about keeping score—it's about **mutual effort, maintenance, and awareness**. It's the golden thread that weaves trust, respect, and love into every relationship we hold dear. Whether with family, friends, or romantic partners, **when we give as much as we receive, relationships become fulfilling, empowering, and deeply rewarding**.

So, take a moment to reflect: Are your relationships balanced? Are you giving and receiving in equal measure? If not, it may be time to reset expectations and nurture relationships that truly honour reciprocity.

The Power of Reciprocity is the foundation of meaningful relationships. After all, the strongest connections are built when both hearts meet halfway.

This is Anna, Thinking Out Loud!

I Ain't Mad at Ya

I ain't mad at Ya—for not knowing better, for not doing better when you should have, for not understanding, for not listening to spoken and unspoken negative messages.

I aint' mad at Ya for not knowing what to do.

For doing what you shouldn't have.

For the mistakes, the missteps, or the moments of uncertainty.

For being uninformed, for acting on impulse, or for making choices you later regretted.

For causing yourself harm, for not recognising your worth, and for falling into the same unhealthy patterns over and over again.

Life doesn't come with a manual, and wisdom isn't born—it's learned.

So, no, I ain't mad at Ya. Growth takes time, and every misstep is just a lesson in disguise.

You are pardoned for it all.

You were in pain. You lost control. You were suffering. You were in darkness. You hadn't healed from your past.

I'm speaking to all the Sistas who lost themselves, who gave up on themselves, who let fear take the place of self-love.

Now, the real work begins. **Forgiving yourself.**

I see you. I feel you.

I used to be you.

"We may encounter many defeats, but we must never be defeated."

—*Maya Angelou*

This is Anna, Thinking Out Loud!

Melanin Queen

She is the Queen,

She is the One,

She is the Mother,

She is the Sun.

She is the Earth,

She is the Moon,

She is the Stars,

She is the Bloom.

She is the Rain,

She is the Pain,

She is the one who breaks all of the Chains.

She is Love

She is Strength,

She is Grace,

The Empress, the Duchess,

The Lioness in her place.

She leads the Tribe,

She is the Vibe!

Queen, straighten your crown.

Walk purposefully in your glory,

And shine bright in your Queendom.

Only step aside from your throne for a true King—

A King who nurtures, uplifts, protects and honours your greatness,

Elevating you higher and higher.

This is Anna, Thinking Out Loud!

Fuel for the Soul: Finding Strength in Words

If you're struggling with challenges that are affecting your self-worth, remember that you are not alone. Across the world, countless individuals have faced similar hardships—and many have shared their wisdom through inspiring words.

Comfort and strength can be found in song lyrics that resonate with us, quotes we stumble upon, the words of personal heroes, spoken word poetry, or scripture. Inspiration is all around us if we take the time to listen, read, and reflect.

Here are just a few powerful expressions that have uplifted me on my own journey of discovery.

"The greatest glory in living lies not in never failing, but in rising every time we fail."

—*Nelson Mandela*

"Things turn out the best for the people who make the best of the way things turn out."

—*John Wooden, American basketball coach*

"Educating the mind without educating the heart is no education at all."

"Love does not begin and end the way we seem to think it does. Love is a battle, love is a war; love is a growing up."

—James Baldwin

"To teach a person to love you to capacity, first show them how much you love yourself! After all, we should all lead by example."

—Annette R. Fraser

"If your heart is broken, make art with the pieces."

—Shane Koyczan

"Character cannot be developed in peace and quiet. Only through experience of trial and suffering can the soul be strengthened, ambition inspired, and success achieved."

—Robert Louis Stevenson

"If you have no confidence in self, you are twice defeated in the race of life."

—Marcus Garvey

"The time is always right to do what is right."

—Dr. Martin Luther King, Jr.

"Courage doesn't always roar. Sometimes courage is the quiet voice at the end of the day, saying, "I will try again tomorrow."

—*Mary Anne Radmacher*

Do you have any powerful expressions that have been momentous to you? List them here:

_____
_____
_____
_____
_____
_____
_____
_____

This is Anna, Thinking Out Loud!

MY Self-Worth

I am admired and despised,

I am liked and disliked,

I am loved by many and hated by a few.

Either way, I'm delighted to take up so much space in your

conscious and unconscious minds.

My desire is to leave positivity and kindness along my journey,

But let's be clear…

My worth is not up for negotiation—

By you, by anyone.

I alone will dictate my worth.

I don't belong to you. I belong to me!

And any negative thoughts of me can never hold me captive.

They say small minds cannot comprehend big spirits—

Well, my big spirit disturbs small minds and unsettles their

demons.

But that's not a "me" problem, that's a "them" problem.

Let them cower to their demons; I stand tall in my divine truth.

Ladies – Own your worth unapologetically, and embrace the power of standing boldly in your truth.

"I can be changed by what happens to me. But I refuse to be reduced by it."

—*Maya Angelou*

This is Anna, Thinking Out Loud!

Repeat After Me

Success comes with consistency.

Every step forward, no matter how small, builds the foundation of greatness. I show up for myself every single day.

I absolutely believe that I will make it.

Doubt has no place in my mind—I know my potential, and I trust the journey. My success is inevitable.

No challenge will make me unstoppable.

Obstacles are not roadblocks; they are stepping stones. I rise, I conquer, and I keep going—If I fall down, I get back up again.

I remain focused on my goals, even in arduous times.

Storms may come, but they will not shake my vision. I adapt, I persist, and I thrive.

I won't stop, I will keep moving, I will absolutely see results.
Quitting is not an option. My determination is unwavering, and my results are undeniable.

My desires are absolutely on route to me.

The universe aligns in my favour. What I seek is already seeking me, and I welcome it with open arms.

I attract financial success effortlessly.

Abundance flows to me in expected and unexpected ways. **Wealth is my birthright, and I claim it without hesitation.**

I am deeply in love with the woman I am becoming. I honour myself, my journey, and my growth. **I am powerful, radiant, and unapologetically me.** I do not shrink—I shine.

This is Anna, Thinking Out Loud!

Why Are You Waiting, Sis?

Why are you still waiting on that man, Sis?

Is fear telling you he's the only one who'll ever want you?

What's keeping you from seeing your own worth?

Does the way he treats you feel right?

Are your basic needs even being met?

When was the last time he took you out—

a romantic dinner, a picnic in the park,

a slow walk by the river, hand in hand?

When was the last time you spent time together, just the two of
you?

When did he last cook a meal for you,

in return for all the meals you've made for him?

Does he eat at your home every day,

But never put shopping in your fridge?

When was the last time he showed you non-sexual intimacy—

forehead kisses, sofa cuddles, touches that make you feel seen?

Has he ever truly matched your effort?

You haven't felt loved in a while, have you?

So let me ask again—if he's been lacking all this time,

Why are you still waiting on that man to meet your needs Sis?

The questions have been asked.

Now find your answer—and take action Sis!

This is Anna, Thinking Out Loud!

Stay Present

Don't dwell on the past—you've already left it behind.

Don't chase the future—it hasn't arrived yet.

If *"What if"* and *"If only"* thoughts keep replaying in your mind, change the question—make it one that leads to action, not regret.

Keep asking yourself the following:

1. What evidence is there for that thought?
2. What evidence is there against that thought?
3. If you were to think differently, what would be the outcome?

All you have is this moment. **Make it count.**

Pay attention to staying present in the here & now, and soon enough, your mind will be uncluttered, and any Low Mood or Anxiety will dissipate, leaving you feeling lighter and more at peace!

This is Anna, Thinking Out Loud!

The 'M' Things to Master

o **Your Mouth**—because your words shape your world.

o **Your Mindfulness**—because presence is power.

o **Your Money**—because control over it means freedom.

o **Your Mood**—because energy is contagious.

o **Your Maturity**—because wisdom elevates you.

o **Your Majesty**—because owning your worth changes everything.

It starts with You. It ends with You.

What do you need to Master?

How will you know it's working?

_____   _____

_____   _____

_____   _____

_____   _____

_____   _____

This is Anna, Thinking Out Loud!

Do You Have Something to Say....

Make sure that you are comfortable,

Are you hungry, too hot, too cold, too tired, too angry. Ask yourself these questions before words leave your mouth...

Is what I'm about to say actually **Correct** or is it about how I am feeling emotionally?

Is what I'm about to say actually **Compulsory,** or am I projecting my own negative thoughts & emotions?

Is what I'm about to say actually **Mindful**- could I be feeling anxious, resentful or annoyed.

Does it actually have to be **uttered** - Is there a positive outcome that I want to achieve?

Does it actually have to be **verbalised by Me** – Are you directly involved or impacted?

Does it actually have to be **articulated by Me in this Moment** - Is this an appropriate time or place?

Just remember, **first** comes the **Thoughts**, then comes the **Feelings** and then comes the **Behaviour**. If you have something to say, you must take responsibility for all of these factors before you speak things into existence.

This is Anna, Thinking Out Loud!

Don't let Your attachment to the past be greater than Your commitment to the future!

Honesty -v- Integrity

Honesty = Telling the Truth

Honesty means not lying. If your partner asks you a direct question, and you give them a truthful answer, you're being honest. But honesty alone doesn't mean you're sharing everything that's relevant—it just means you're not actively deceiving.

For example, if you went to lunch with an ex and your partner asks, "Did you have lunch with anyone today?" and you answer, "Yeah, I grabbed a quick bite," you're technically being honest. But you're also leaving out an important detail.

Transparency = Openly Sharing What Matters

Transparency goes beyond just telling the truth when asked. It means proactively sharing things that could affect your partner or your relationship—things they'd want to know. It's about creating trust by making sure they never have to wonder what you're *not* saying.

Using the same example, if you were transparent, you'd say, "Yeah, I had lunch with my ex today. It was unplanned, but I wanted to let you know." That way, your partner doesn't have to dig for the full truth, and they feel included in what's happening in your life.

Why Transparency is So Important

1. **It Builds Trust** – If your partner knows you're always upfront with them, they won't have to second-guess your words or actions. Trust isn't just about not lying—it's about not leaving room for doubt.

2. **It Prevents Misunderstandings** – If your partner finds out about something later, they may feel like you hid it, even if that wasn't your intention.

3. **It Strengthens Emotional Intimacy** – Being open with each other fosters a deeper connection. Transparency shows that you respect your partner enough to share things that matter.

4. **It Avoids Unnecessary Conflicts** – A lack of transparency often leads to suspicion, insecurity, or resentment. Open communication keeps the relationship healthy.

When you're sharing an intimate moment in conversation with your partner, friend or foe, pause and take a moment to consider and ask yourself: Am I speaking from a place of honesty or transparency?

In short- Honesty answers questions. **Transparency** eliminates the need to ask them.

This is Anna, Thinking Out Loud!

167

The Saviour Complex: When Healing Others Leaves You Broken

There's a strange emotional magnetism that can draw us toward people who are emotionally damaged or deeply flawed—people whose pain is almost visible. And for some of us, it's not entirely accidental. It's something deeper... something we don't always see in ourselves until the pattern repeats.

It's what many refer to as a *saviour complex*—the unconscious urge to heal, fix, or be the light in someone else's darkness.

At first, it can look like love.

It can feel like compassion.

It often starts with empathy and patience—but underneath, there's something else quietly unfolding: an inner belief that *maybe your love can be the thing that changes them.*

You see the red flags. You notice the emotional unavailability, the unresolved trauma, the lack of self-awareness—or worse, signs of manipulation. You're not blind to it. But you accommodate. You tell yourself it's temporary. That they'll grow, soften, open up. You give them time and space. You monitor. You hope.

Sometimes, we don't speak up about our concerns early on—not because we don't see them, but because we're watching to see whether the behaviour is a one-off or something more rooted. We "wait it out," not realising that each time we overlook something, we're unconsciously teaching the other person what we're willing to accept.

And then somewhere down the line, we burn out.

We're exhausted from holding up both ends of the emotional rope.

And the very things we noticed in the beginning—the very traits we tried to be patient with—become the reasons the relationship begins to unravel.

The truth is: what you identify early on in a connection often holds the seed of how things will eventually fall apart.

Love is not meant to be a project.

You are not a rehab centre for people who refuse to heal themselves.

And no matter how strong or kind or capable you are, it is not your job to be someone's emotional crutch.

Healing others should never come at the expense of your own peace.

And relationships should be rooted in mutual growth, not silent sacrifice.

So if you've found yourself repeatedly forming attachments with people who need saving, maybe it's time to ask:

What part of me believes that being loved means being needed?

What am I trying to prove by staying silent about my needs?

What would love feel like if I didn't have to earn it through suffering?

You deserve a love that sees *you*—not just your capacity to carry someone else's wounds.

Let this be your reminder:

You can care.

You can empathise.

You can even walk beside someone in their healing.

But you don't have to carry them.

Not at the cost of yourself.

This is Anna, thinking out loud.

I'm LOUD With It!

I **refuse** to water myself down just to make myself more palatable for others. If you find me too much, too loud, too vibrant— **that's your issue, not mine.** I will never shrink myself to fit into someone else's comfort zone. If my loud presence disturbs you, you have **many** options at your disposal—walk away, don't engage, remove yourself from my space. But what I will **not** do is contort myself into something unnatural just to appease your fragile sensibilities. I'm speaking to everyone who has ever told me to tone it down!

I **speak with energy, with fire, with presence**—that's who I am. If you can't handle the volume, then go sit in another space. But don't you dare expect me to silence myself for you. If you find me indigestible, **go ahead and choke on your own vomit**— I won't let that ruin my appetite and it won't stop me from enjoying my meal!

Let's be very clear, I will never tiptoe through my own life just because you think I should be quieter. **Every step I take will be heard. Every move I make will be felt.** And I promise you—**I'll make sure you hear every single m#therf*k"*g step!**

*This is Anna, Thinking Out **Loud Loud Loud!***

Cultivating Inner Calm in a Chaotic World

Emotions play a crucial role in our lives. The key to emotional well-being lies in recognising, understanding, and managing these emotions effectively. By becoming more aware of how you feel, you can learn to navigate your emotions in healthier ways and express them more constructively.

One way to build emotional awareness is by identifying different emotions and reflecting on your personal experiences with them. Taking note of when and how these emotions arise can help you gain a deeper understanding of your emotional patterns.

Feelings of **despair and despondency** often accompany difficult or tragic circumstances. When overwhelmed by these emotions, it may feel as though the future no longer holds promise, leading to a loss of motivation and a sense of giving up. Identifying and Acknowledging these feelings is the first step toward regaining perspective and finding renewed hope.

Shame arises from a sense of embarrassment or self-judgment, often triggered by the belief that one has acted in a dishonourable or improper way. It is a deeply self-conscious emotion that can lead to

172

harsh self-criticism. Learning to separate actions from self-worth can help in overcoming shame.

Guilt emerges when you feel responsible for a perceived wrongdoing, whether real or imagined. While guilt can serve as a moral compass, it can also become overwhelming and irrational, leading to unnecessary self-punishment. Finding a balanced perspective and self-forgiveness is essential to moving forward.

Anxiety manifests as nervousness, unease, or persistent worry about uncertain outcomes. It can create a sense of inner turmoil and make challenges seem insurmountable. Understanding the triggers of anxiety and developing coping mechanisms can help restore a sense of control and resilience.

Reflect on recent events, situations, or thoughts that may have triggered your feelings of despair/hopelessness/shame/guilt/anxiety. Write them down, even if they seem insignificant.

_____
_____
_____
_____
_____
_____

Consider if feelings of despair/hopelessness/shame/guilt/anxiety are a recurring pattern in your life.

Have you felt this way before? If so, when and in what situations?

_____

_____

_____

_____

Describe any symptoms you experience when feeling despair/ hopelessness/ shame/ guilt/ anxiety.

This could include fatigue, sadness, isolation, loss of interest, etc.

_____

_____

_____

_____

_____

_____

_____

Write down some of the specific thoughts or self-talk that accompany your feelings of despair/ hopelessness/ shame/ guilt/ anxiety. For example, "I can't do anything right," or "Nothing ever works out for me."

_____

_____

_____

_____

_____

_____

_____

_____

How do your feelings of despair/ hopelessness/ shame/ guilt/ anxiety affect your daily life?

Consider relationships, work or school, self-care, and overall well-being.

_____

_____

_____

_____

_____

_____

_____

Reflect on the strategies you currently use to cope with despair/hopelessness/shame/guilt/anxiety.

Are these strategies helpful or unhelpful in managing your feelings? Why?

_____

_____

_____

_____

_____

_____

_____

_____

List the people in your life who you can turn to for support when you feel despair/ hopelessness/ shame/guilt/anxiety. How comfortable are you reaching out to them?

_____

_____

_____

_____

_____

_____

_____

Describe any self-care practices or activities that you find comforting or helpful when you feel despair/ hopelessness/ shame/ guilt/anxiety. This could include exercise, relaxation techniques, hobbies, or spending time with loved ones.

_____

_____

_____

_____

_____

_____

Consider what a hopeful future might look like for you. What changes or improvements would you like to see in your life? Are there any goals you want to set for yourself?

_____

_____

_____

_____

_____

_____

_____

Reflect on your personal strengths and positive qualities. What are some things you appreciate about yourself, even when you feel despair/hopelessness/shame/guilt/anxiety?

_____

_____

_____

_____

_____

_____

_____

Next, follow the steps outlined above.

1. Argue the Opposite. Is there evidence that things might work out better than you expect?

How might things get better? Focus on the potential positives to open up possibilities.

_____

_____

_____

_____

_____

_____

_____

_____

2. Consider What You Gain When You Feel despair/ hopelessness/ shame/ guilt/ anxiety.

Be honest and specific.

_____

_____

_____

_____

_____

_____

_____

_____

3. Consider What You Gain from Developing Hope. How might your life change? What would you be doing differently if you felt hopeful?

_____

_____

_____

_____

_____

_____

_____

4. Engage in Problem-Solving. Focus on potential solutions and brainstorm ideas. See if you can come up with as many strategies as you can. If a problem seems unsolvable, consider how to change how you feel about the problem.

_____

_____

_____

_____

_____

_____

5. Talk to a Trusted Friend or Family Member. Who will you talk to? When?

_____

_____

_____

_____

_____

6. Develop a Plan. After you have come up with solutions or brainstormed ideas—alone or with others—create a plan and decide what to do. If plan A fails to work, identify a plan B.

Plan A

_____

_____

_____

_____

_____

_____

_____

Plan B

_____

_____

_____

_____

_____

_____

_____

Resources used:

_____

_____

_____

_____

_____

_____

_____

7. Take Action. After you have identified your plan, take action—one step at a time. What will you do? By what date?

_____

_____

_____

_____

_____

_____

_____

Deliberations on This Piece of Work

What was challenging about this task? Be detailed.

_____

_____

181

_____

_____

_____

_____

_____

_____

Did anything surprise you about this activity? If so, describe.

_____

_____

_____

_____

_____

_____

Did you feel more hopeful after completing this task? Why or why not?

_____

_____

_____

_____

_____

_____

What did you learn from this task?

_____

_____

_____

_____

_____

_____

_____

_____

This is Anna, Thinking Out Loud!

She is Unbreakable. Unshaken. Unmatched. And Undeniably Equipped.

For every boardroom she's walked into, every door she's had to pry open, she carries the lessons, not the labels.

They told her to wait her turn -

but she's *Not Waiting. Not Wavering. Not Losing. Just Winning—With Receipts.*

In spaces where they tried to dim her light, she showed up brighter.

Bold by Nature. Brilliant by Design. Battle-tested and Built to Lead.

Leadership is not a position she hopes for—it's a presence she *embodies.*

In love, she doesn't shrink to fit or stretch to be chosen.

Never Silenced. Never Settled. Always Seen. Always Ready.

She knows now that love isn't earned through endurance—it's received in alignment.

And when it comes to Self-Worth?

She wears it like skin—no need for permission, no desire for perfection.

Too Wise to Be Shaken. Too Rare to Be Rivalled. **Too Real to Be Dismissed.**

Because this woman?

She's not becoming powerful—

She's finally *owning* that she always was!

This is my Manifesto… Now You write Yours!

This is Anna, Thinking Out Loud!

A Final Word...

Own Your Power, Speak Your Truth

I've always been told that I have a big mouth and a big attitude. Some might take that as an insult, but not me—I embrace it fully and stand tall in it. Why? Because it's true, and more importantly, it's a gift. My voice, my attitude, and my unapologetic presence exist for a purpose: to advocate, uplift, and empower others.

I have an insatiable curiosity and let's be honest—I love to talk! That's exactly why I started *Thinking Out Loud*. I'm not here as a polished, traditional writer. I didn't set out to craft the perfect prose. I simply wanted a space—a journal, a movement—to express myself, to challenge perspectives, to ignite motivation, and to empower women to stand fully in their own power.

At the end of the day, I can't force anyone to see the value in my words, nor can I make you appreciate the truths I've shared. But if even one thought, one idea, or one moment of reflection from this book sparks something within you, then I've done what I set out to do.

I said it earlier, and I'll say it again: Remember, My goal is Growth, my Desire is Empowerment, and my religion is Love. I have shared all of this with my raw insights on life, love, and self-worth, weaving together wisdom, therapeutic reflections, and empowering exercises designed to help you **own your story and stand in your power**.

Whether you're overcoming obstacles, reclaiming your confidence, or simply looking for a reminder of how **worthy and capable you truly are**, these words are your companion on the journey.

This is for the woman who has stayed quiet for too long.

This is for the woman ready to take up space.

This is for *You*.

Take what fuels your soul, run with it, and above all, own your truth—boldly and fearlessly. Because the power has always been yours. And really—when you think about it—it *is* just that simple.

What if the key to your power was simply **giving yourself permission to speak your truth**?

Are you ready to start Thinking Out Loud?

-End-

I'm Her... She's Me... I Love Her... She Loves Me...Walking in My Purpose!

This is more than a guide—it's a reflection, a reminder, and a call for every woman to step fully into your power.

Through these pages, you'll find words that uplift, exercises that heal, and reflections that remind you of your worth. This journey is about self-discovery, self-love, and stepping boldly into the life you were meant to live.

You are not alone in your growth. You are seen, you are valued, and you are capable of more than you ever imagined. This is for the woman who knows there is more, who refuses to settle, and who is ready to reclaim her voice.

www.ingramcontent.com/pod-product-compliance
Lightning Source LLC
Chambersburg PA
CBHW051151120626
46547CB00012B/1034